# Praise for *Buried Dreams*

"I was one of thousands who followed Lindsey and Kevin Dennis on their journey of joy, dashed hope, devastating loss, then courageous trust not once but twice. Their honesty and vulnerability were remarkable and inspiring through such difficult times. Their willingness to continue to believe God's love and goodness as their anticipation of new life turned into the death of their dreams will help many to navigate great losses in their own lives. You will weep with them and stand amazed at the depth of their faith. You will be touched—and changed."

—***Judy Douglass***, writer, speaker, director at Women's Resources at Cru

"Death is all wrong. God never intended that we die, and one day death will be no more. But until then everyone lives with its shadow. Lindsey has been to death's door with two newborn daughters and, there, has found the wonder of God's all sufficiency, His comforting presence, and the hope He alone can offer us in our darkest days. Adoration, worship, and peace arise in our hearts when we experience the good He can bring out of devastating loss."

—***Barbara Rainey***, author of *A Symphony in the Dark* and *Letters to My Daughters*; founder of Ever Thine Home

"Lindsey captures hard-won truths found in the places of loss, grief, and questions without answers and weaves in lessons learned through her study of God's Word. This book offers comfort and hope to those who walk the road of suffering and offers insights for those who seek to be companions on the journey. A beautiful tribute to life, community, and ultimately the God who can be trusted."

—***Vivian Mabuni***, speaker and author of *Warrior in Pink*

"This book will make you smile, cry, and laugh and make you fist pump for how big our God is to use such tiny little girls to share His story. Sophie and Dasah were such remarkable little girls. I think they got it from their brave mommy who has blessed us all by sharing their story with us. Lindsey Dennis will captivate your heart with her bravery, knowledge of the Word, and sincere love for our Lord."

—***Jennafer White***, author of *Be Love*

"In all of my life so far I have never traveled with a couple who have more beautifully embraced grief in unthinkable tragedy and brutality of life while simultaneously fully embracing hope in the beauty of God's redemption story. Kevin and

Lindsey have lived between worlds in the profound and impossible space where grief and hope coexist. You will find in these pages a true story that your heart will deeply connect with and where you will be profoundly transformed."

—**Renaut van der Riet**, lead pastor at Mosaic Church

"Expect to be completely drawn into this true and life-changing story! Unhindered vulnerability, honest thoughts, questions, and feelings will be raised. Then, just when you start wondering how to address them, the truth is brought into the discussion to guide you forward. Every chapter will leave you wanting to read the next as you discover that there is hope in the midst of buried dreams."

—**Michael Parrott**, DMin, founder of His Heart, My Heart Transformations

"What a beautiful book. And I say beautiful because there is a special beauty to hope and confidence in God that shines in and through the darkest places of life. There is beauty in the love expressed, beauty in the words chosen, and beauty in truths taken hold of and offered to all in this book."

—**Nancy Guthrie**, author of *Hearing Jesus Speak Into Your Sorrow*

"What does it look like for God to meet you in your darkest night, your deepest ravine? You hold the answer in your hands. This story delicately holds hope and lament, fear and faith, and life and death together. And isn't that the story of the cross? An invitation to know joy in the center of suffering? I didn't want to miss a single page of how these buried dreams became living treasures. My faith grew deeper because of the brutal and yet beautiful depths of this journey. Thank you, Lindsey, for courageously telling your story."

—**Amy Seiffert**, author of *Chin Up: Wearing Grace, Strength, and Dignity When Motherhood Unravels Our Souls*

"Lindsey Dennis is the real deal. She is a woman who has walked the journey always with a heart steadfast in the Lord and His promises despite the grief, pain, and loss of the journey. Sisterhood had the privilege of hosting Lindsey as our keynote speaker in Australia when she was in the middle of this journey. The message she shared was inspiring and gave hope to so many women. I know that every single person who reads her words will be inspired, encouraged, and renewed in what it means to live with a hope that does not disappoint. I feel so blessed to call Lindsey a friend and it has been a joy and privilege to walk with her and be a part of her journey."

—**Karen Doyle**, author, speaker and cofounder of Sisterhood Womens Movement Australia and Choicez Media.

# Buried Dreams

*From* Devastating Loss *to* Unimaginable Hope

## LINDSEY R. DENNIS

*Abingdon Press / Nashville*

BURIED DREAMS
FROM DEVASTATING LOSS TO UNIMAGINABLE HOPE

Copyright © 2018 by Abingdon Press

**Library of Congress Cataloging-in-Publication Data has been requested.**

*ISBN 978-1-5018-6911-2*

"The Mist Will Rise," *Figures of the True* by Amy Carmichael, © 1938 The Dohnavur Fellowship. Used by permission of CLC Publications. May not be further reproduced. All rights reserved.

*Candles in the Dark* by Amy Carmichael, © 1981 The Dohnavur Fellowship. Used by permission of CLC Publications. May not be further reproduced. All rights reserved.

"Make Me Thy Fuel," *Toward Jerusalem* by Amy Carmichael, © 1936 The Dohnavur Fellowship. Used by permission of CLC Publications. May not be further reproduced. All rights reserved.

"We Conquer by His Song," *Toward Jerusalem* by Amy Carmichael, © 1936 The Dohnavur Fellowship. Used by permission of CLC Publications. May not be further reproduced. All rights reserved.

Kenneth Padgett, "The Best Is Yet to Come," track 6 of *A Sweet and Bitter Providence* by The Joy Eternal (2011).

Dan Allender, "The Hidden Hope in Lament," Mars Hill Review 1 (1994): 25–38.

Unless noted otherwise, all Scripture taken from the NEW AMERICAN STANDARD BIBLE®, Copyright © 1960,1962,1963,1968,1971, 1972,1973,1975,1977,1995 by The Lockman Foundation. Used by permission.

Scripture taken from the ESV® Bible (The Holy Bible, English Standard Version®). ESV® Text Edition: 2016. Copyright © 2001 by Crossway, a publishing ministry of Good News Publishers. The ESV® text has been reproduced in cooperation with and by permission of Good News Publishers. Unauthorized reproduction of this publication is prohibited. All rights reserved.

Scripture taken from THE HOLY BIBLE, NEW INTERNATIONAL VERSION®, NIV® Copyright © 1973, 1978, 1984, 2011 by Biblica, Inc.® Used by permission. All rights reserved worldwide.

Scripture taken from the New Testament in Modern English by J.B. Phillips copyright © 1960, 1972 J. B. Phillips. Administered by The Archbishops' Council of the Church of England. Used by Permission.

18 19 20 21 22 23 24 25 26 27—10 9 8 7 6 5 4 3 2 1

MANUFACTURED IN THE UNITED STATES OF AMERICA

*For Sophie.*
*For Dasah.*
*You pointed our hearts to Jesus and showed us*
*the greatness of our God.*
*I'm so glad God gave me the gift of being your mommy.*
*You both have my heart, always and forever.*

*For Jaden, Briella, and all the children God*
*may give us in the future.*
*I pray these chapters and all the ones yet to be written would be ones*
*where we would tell generations to come of God's faithfulness to us in*
*each and every page of our lives.*
*You are gracious gifts to me this side of Heaven.*

*Psalm 145:3-5*

# CONTENTS

CONTENTS

*Where are ye, O ye mountains? Not a peak*
*Has looked on me throughout this heavy day.*
*Where is your purple? I see nought but grey;*
*The place you once made glad is cold and bleak.*

*See, wind and sun perform their ministry.*
*Watch the tossed mist shape silver frames of cloud,*
*Until the crags, like friendly faces, crowd*
*To look through clear, large windowpanes at Thee.*

*The sun streams out and shines through wetted leaves,*
*And strikes the fern like golden rust aslant.*
*Hark to the birds; the wood is jubilant,*
*As if the world held nowhere one that grieves.*

*Then, O my heart, be comforted; be strong.*
*The mist will pass; the mountains will remain;*
*The sun will shine; the birds will sing again.*
*In mist, in rain, look up and sing thy song.*

—Amy Carmichael, "The Mist Will Rise"

# ONE

## The Death of Dreams

*One thing I know,*
*God's story never ends with ashes.*
*Nothing is for nothing.*

—Elisabeth Elliot

Our car slowly made its way over the bumpy cobblestone road, canopied by Spanish moss dangling from giant oak trees above, as we passed through the open iron gates.

The road quickly became smooth as we entered the cemetery, but my heart was anything but smooth. We drove past the small rolling hills full of gravesites and up to the top of the little hill in the middle of all the others. There, the tiny white casket with the shell of the body of our firstborn daughter rested.

Earlier in the morning, I sat on our worn chair in the living room of our small second-floor apartment. I looked up at my husband, Kevin, and with weary eyes asked what I realized he would not be able to answer:

"This is the last hardest thing we have to do, right?"

I meant "ever."

Bury our firstborn daughter. We won't ever have to do anything harder than this? Of course, he wouldn't answer the way I hoped he would. He did not hold all knowledge of the future. But that morning, I really wanted him to.

"I don't know," was his response, as he looked at me with kind and knowing eyes.

"But this is the last hardest thing we have to do with our daughter."

His response was clearly not the comfort I was hoping for. His words were void of the security I desired. I wanted to hold onto a hope that our circumstances would never be this hard again. I wanted the surety that God would never ask us to bury another child. Unfortunately that kind of hope is elusive and unstable. For as much as I like to think I can control my circumstances, they are ever-changing and unpredictable. We cannot hope in our circumstances but in the One who is Lord over our circumstances. Easier said than done, right?

Over the course of my life there had been many pivotal moments where I had been brutally awakened to the reality that my hope was in what God would do for me and not in God alone. I would sing, "You are my only hope" from the comfort of my seat on an average Sunday morning. But did I really believe it? Would this hope that would grip me in moments fade away as my day and the week went on? What did Paul mean when he said we have a hope that doesn't disappoint when life can be full of such brutal disappointments (Romans 5:5)?

---

You never expect to bury your dream. But it happens to us all. The day comes and we are paralyzed, staring down at what we never thought could be written into our story.

---

Throughout our lives there are many circumstances where our hope must be reoriented and woven deeper in our hearts. In singleness, in broken relationships, in unmet expectations, in career uncertainty, and now, for me, in the death of our precious child.

⊗⊗⊗

Twenty-two weeks earlier, this new season had begun. Kevin and I had just found out at my twenty-week ultrasound the child I was carrying had a severe, life-limiting condition and would not live long once born. There would be no cure or treatment. And it began a stunning unraveling of our dreams for the child we carried, of our hopes for our family and the future.

And though we were overwhelmed with grief, Kevin and I chose to carry her to term. Her short life captivated the hearts of hundreds and then thousands as a community gathered around us cherishing and celebrating each day she grew in my womb.

Stunned at the magnitude of love that poured out for a child yet to be born, there were no hearts so captivated by love and changed by her life than her daddy's and mine. Those months were rich and full of so many conflicting emotions. There was so much joy in her life amid the many tears that fell in the brutal anticipation of her death.

After forty-two weeks and two days, our firstborn daughter, Sophia Kyla Dennis, entered the world. She arrived with arms stretched wide and the sweetest cries I had ever heard. I delighted in every second she was in my arms.

But how would I bury this child I loved and had so many dreams and hopes for? I did my best not to think of what that day would be like. My heart grew weak even as I tried to anticipate how God would enable us to survive that day.

For no one can prepare you for burying your child, even when you know it is coming. And no one can prepare you for what it will be like to stand in front of a tiny casket and embrace the reality that this child you bore and held and loved would never be in your arms again this side of heaven.

You never expect to bury your dream.

But it happens to us all. The day comes and we are paralyzed, staring down at what we never thought could be written into our story. Pain and tragedy, we realize, are a part of life, but somehow it can appear as though the unexpected will only happen to those around us, not to us.

You didn't think you'd be thirty and single, be unemployed, struggle with infertility, lose a loved one so young, or maybe like me, you never thought you'd have to bury your child. That wasn't in my plans or the story I had dreamed of for my life. But it would be those very places of pain, disappointment, and buried dreams that would become the fertile soil for the hope that doesn't disappoint to rise in my soul.

❊❊❊

As Kevin and I pulled up to the gravesite, several friends gathered around our car. I didn't want to be there. I didn't want my eyes to meet theirs because somehow it made the day a little more real, as if it was indeed all true. I had carried a beautiful baby girl. Her hiccups and kicks had kept me from sleeping and reminded me she was still alive. Hundreds of people helped Kevin and me celebrate her life and make incredible memories with her in the womb. I heard her breathe, held her in my arms, and listened to her sweet cries.

I wanted to relive every moment I had with my little girl as truth but not the last part. Not the part where I said goodbye to her little shell of a body, and not the part where I stood there about to bury her in the ground. This couldn't possibly be the story God had asked me to walk.

That day it seemed as if my story, her story had ended in ashes. In those moments I had forgotten all that God had done in the previous twenty-two weeks. How He had used His people to lift my weary arms and help me celebrate Sophie's short life. I had forgotten the laughter and joy He had brought in the midst of the tears. I wasn't able to see in those moments of such pain, the depth of His goodness and hope He had woven into my heart as I wrestled with this chapter He had written into my story.

In moments where the sorrow of life is often overwhelming, it is easy to lose sight of any goodness beyond the pain. In the months that followed, God drew me back to the aspects of His character He had been rooting in my heart. But on this brutal day when I buried my firstborn daughter, I needed a fresh encounter of hope. It seems daily we need a fresh encounter and reminder of the hope we have. We forget so easily.

It's easier to dwell on the shattered dreams, the unmet expectations, all it appears we've lost and miss the reality that the God who holds the world on its axis holds us in the palm of His hand. We can't see in the loneliness of our grief that those who gather around us in our pain are a reflection of His deep love for us when His love feels far away.

Sitting in the car at the gravesite, fighting to not dwell on my own shattered dreams, a silent prayer rose in my heart as Kevin and I prepared to face the inevitable.

"An infusion of hope today, Lord. Someone please offer me hope because I can't see beyond my pain right now."

---

Suddenly, I'd never seen a more beautiful casket. I'm not sure I would have ever used the words *beautiful* and *casket* in the same sentence. It was a small glimpse of redemption now and redemption to come when the Savior breathes life into every broken and dying piece of our heart. It's what He does. It's what He came to do—a gentle reminder that there is no pain so deep that our God cannot redeem.

---

My sunglasses on, my head hung down in despair, unrelenting tears a slow and steady stream on my cheeks, and the pain just hanging in the air, I slowly stepped out of the car.

A few steps later my pastor, Renaut Van Der Riet, was by my side, a comforting smile on his face and an answer to my prayer on his lips.

Tall (taller than Kevin, which is quite tall since my husband is 6'4"), with dark hair and a slight South African accent, he had a commanding and comforting presence. Kevin and I met with him often throughout our journey with Sophie and always walked out of his office with lightness in our step, as if we had just been asked to be a part of the most beautiful and redemptive story. I couldn't wrap my mind around how he did it, but he had a way of breathing the hope of Christ into the darkest moments. Today was no different.

"I wish we were not here today, but I have to tell you as I was driving over I became so excited for today. Not for what today is, but for how God may speak to you both and lift our eyes to something greater," he said with joy and hope written on his face I wished was written on mine.

"Excited for the day?" He was the only one who could get away with such words. And only God had heard the prayer I had prayed and answered in such a profound way. Someone to offer me the hope that God would do something in my heart and lift my eyes to the Anchor for my soul I desperately needed as the weight of my grief was about to swallow me whole.

The words Renaut spoke at the gravesite that day held the hope and promise of heaven, as ten of our close family and friends sat underneath a small green tent. Colorful flowers cascaded over tall white stands on either side of Sophie's little casket, where a large bouquet of pink, blue, white, purple, and orange balloons was tied to a chair and reaching for the bright blue sky above.

Renaut gave a picture of the glorious future when all will be made new and the sorrows in this life will make the joy of heaven sweeter. Smiles began to be mixed with tears as my eyes were turned heavenward.

After Renaut spoke, Kevin and I gathered around Sophie's little white casket that, to be honest, was quite ugly. I felt bad about that. Fortunately we had brought pink and blue paint so Kevin and I could put our hand-prints on top of it, filling it with color and life. We knelt beside it, painting each of our hands and then pressing those messy colorful palms onto the top of her little casket.

We laughed at the mess of it all, the paint all over our fingers, the imperfect handprints just a few inches from where our daughter's little body lay. I think Sophie would have liked that.

We placed butterfly stickers, each filled with short notes to Sophie from family and friends, all over that ugly little casket, transforming it into a beautiful sea of love written in color.

Suddenly, I'd never seen a more beautiful casket. I'm not sure I would have ever used the words *beautiful* and *casket* in the same sentence. It was a small glimpse of redemption now and redemption to come when the Savior breathes life into every broken and dying piece of our heart. It's what He does. It's what He came to do—a gentle reminder that there is no pain so deep that our God cannot redeem.

The prophet Isaiah testifies to this promise of redemption, pointing us to the one who would come: "To comfort all who mourn; to grant to those who mourn in Zion—to give them a beautiful headdress instead of ashes, the oil of gladness instead of mourning, the garment of praise instead of a faint spirit; that they may be called oaks of righteousness, the planting of the LORD, that he may be glorified" (Isaiah 61:2-3 ESV).

The savior God's people were hoping would come would display all the beauty Isaiah spoke of, and this is now our Savior who has come. His promise of restoration is still playing out in the hearts of countless men and women who come to call Him their Savior too.

His name is Jesus, and our journey with Sophie was just the beginning of knowing with greater depth and awe the One that makes beauty out of ashes. He was the One whose promise of restoration was being played out in my life in unseen and unexpected ways.

> I imagine you feel it, too, in your own buried
> dreams, in learning how to adjust to a life
> where what you'd hoped it would include is
> missing—in learning how to embrace and
> live with the often-daily tension of the joy
> and pain that now exists.

We gathered around Sophie's casket, me in a flowing white dress covered in butterflies, Kevin in a baby blue shirt and khaki pants, my mom and several other friends clothed in color. Arm in arm we sang through our sorrow the words in that great old hymn "How Great Thou Art." The lyrics point to the splendor of our God, the hope of the cross, and the hope of the day when Christ comes and we are taken to our true home. And that day we will see with eyes wide open and full clarity the greatness of our God in all His glory and splendor as we sing, "My Savior God, to Thee, How great thou art."

Hope filled my heart as I stood there and longed for the day when all would be made new. It was as if I understood the words to those lyrics for the first time. Unspeakable joy in the midst of my tears at the mere thought of what that day would be like—to see Jesus face-to-face, to see my daughter, for all this pain to be redeemed. Her life and now death were giving me a deeper experience of joy—joy not apart from my tears but enhanced because of my tears.

At that time, I did not know how many more tears would still fall, how much joy would seem to be shrouded by mystery, and how much more grief we would bear in that coming year.

Fourteen months later Kevin and I would be standing there again, next to the headstone of our first daughter, with the little casket of our second daughter before us, about to bury her as well. It would be another devastating goodbye. And my dreams for motherhood, for how my life would unfold, would come to a crashing halt.

Buried.

Two daughters in the ground.

How could it be? The depth to which my dreams died the day I stood at the gravesite for a second time cannot be put into words. What hope could rise from not one but two graves?

These precious dreams that I had for my life had not only been unrealized but utterly shattered right before my eyes. And I felt as if God Himself had little concern for the devastation such loss would leave. How much pain can the soul endure? How much light can break through layer upon layer of darkness? When will the night end? When will the dawn of hope arise? What beauty could rise from these ashes?

❋❋❋

If I told you that this story you are about to read will be an unpacking of everything I have just written above, you would rightfully conclude that what you are about to read is filled with devastating loss and unbearable heartbreak. These chapters in my story are very much a sad story, but they are also so much more than a sad story. For the sadness has revealed the joy, and the grave has displayed the resurrection hope we were created for, promised, and given.

Our culture likes to categorize stories—happy or sad, joyful or painful. It seems we are uncomfortable living in the tension of the joy and the ache our stories, and ultimately this world, hold. When faced with tragedy, this is what begins to take place in the heart of the one in pain. There is a constant collision of joy and pain. But truth be told, even without what we would define as tragedy in our lives, we all ache in some way for the things in our lives that are not what we thought they would be, that are not as we know they should be.

I imagine you feel it, too, in your own buried dreams, in learning how to adjust to a life where what you'd hoped it would include is missing—in learning how to embrace and live with the often-daily tension of the joy and pain that now exists.

And it is in these places of tension where transformation has begun in my life.

For in between all the bottles of tears I have filled, in between each buried dream, in between all of the astounding shattering of my soul, there has been hope—hope that has indeed arisen in the darkness. Hope that has been forged in the very midst of my deep pain. Hope that breaks through the darkness and leads to joy and peace in ways that only darkness can reveal, because of the unlikely and unexpected companions of sorrow and suffering.

---

It seems a strange path, to be taken through the wilderness into the darkness and be given the companions of Sorrow and Suffering as part of the way to find the places our hearts long for and ultimately the person our hearts long for.

---

One of my favorite books is an allegory by Hannah Hurnard titled *Hinds' Feet on High Places*. It has been a beautiful picture for me of the strange ways that God allows sorrow and suffering to be pathways to know the greatness of His love and hope more fully.

In her book, Hurnard tells the story of a young girl named Much-Afraid who is called by the Good Shepherd to go to the High Places where fear is transformed by love, and the Good Shepherd turns her weakness into strength.

It is an allegory inspired by the words of the prophet Habakkuk, a little book toward the end of the Old Testament, where the prophet makes the bold declaration amid stunning sorrow he sees and experiences: "Yet I will exult in the LORD, I will rejoice in the God of my salvation. The Lord GOD is my strength, and He has made my feet like hinds' feet, and makes me walk on my high places" (Habakkuk 3:18-19).

In Hurnard's book, Much-Afraid is struggling with her own losses. She is lame in one leg and tormented daily by her relatives. She desires to go to the High Places with the Good Shepherd, but fear runs deep as she anticipates the dangers involved in leaving her home.

---

Suffering is never wasted. It has purpose and is an integral and, yes, even a necessary part of the journey of a believer to taste the fullness of the joy of Christ.

---

Can she trust the Good Shepherd to take her there without harm?

As she sheepishly and slowly learns to follow Him, much to her dismay, He gives her the companions of Sorrow and Suffering. Upon hearing the names of her new companions, she exclaims:

> "I can't go with them," she gasped. "I can't! I can't! O my Lord Shepherd, why do You do this to me? How can I travel in their company? It is more than I can bear. You tell me that the mountain way itself is so steep and difficult that I cannot climb it alone. Then why, oh why, must you make Sorrow and Suffering my companions? Couldn't You have given Joy and Peace to go with me, to strengthen me and encourage me and help me on the difficult way? I never thought You would do this to me!" And she burst into tears.[1]

This was much like my response to God as I walked through carrying two little girls, loving, cherishing, and celebrating them for nine months in the womb, only to say goodbye too quickly.

*I never thought you would do this to me!* my heart also exclaimed to my Good Shepherd. *How could this be the way to know You, Lord?*

Sorrow and Suffering had become my companions, too, and I could not have known—much like Much-Afraid—how they would become the way in which my heart would be carried to the High Places. I, too, would learn to walk on the heights and see Sorrow and Suffering transformed into Joy and Peace.

It seems a strange path, to be taken through the wilderness into the darkness and be given the companions of Sorrow and Suffering as part of the way to find the places our hearts long for and ultimately the person our hearts long for. Paul speaks often of this in the New Testament. To the believers in Rome he says, "we can be full of joy here and now even in our trials and troubles. Taken in the right spirit these very things will give us patient endurance; this in turn will develop a mature character, and a character of this sort produces a steady hope, a hope that will never disappoint us" (Romans 5:3-5 PHILLIPS).

How could this be true when I feel so utterly disappointed? What is the hope that Paul speaks of that can only be found through the progression of suffering, endurance, character, and hope? Paul speaks of these truths again to the Corinthians: "For momentary, light affliction is producing for us an eternal weight of glory far beyond all comparison, while we look not at the things which are seen, but at the things which are not seen; for the things which are seen are temporal, but the things which are not seen are eternal" (2 Corinthians 4:17-18).

Light. Momentary.

Surely the affliction and suffering I've experienced, watched others experience, and perhaps you have experienced would not be described that way. And yet, here is how Paul describes it. There was no way to get away from it. These words he chose were not a mistake. For they were the very words of God spoken through Paul.

And when I looked up, when I looked at unseen things, when I looked at my circumstances through the lens of God and eternity, I observed something different altogether. For God was at work in the darkest moments of my life, doing what only He was able to do to draw my heart to the reality of His glory, His love, and His worthiness of my life. Suffering is never wasted. It has purpose and is an integral and, yes, even a necessary part of the journey of a believer to taste the fullness of the joy of Christ.

Jesus says as He's preparing his followers for his death, "Truly, truly, I say to you, unless a grain of wheat falls into the earth and dies, it remains alone; but if it dies, it bears much fruit" (John 12:24).

Death for life. Life in death. It's the way of the Cross. It's the way of the people of the Cross, and it's the way to know the Person on the Cross.

⊠⊠⊠

Standing in front of that little colorful casket of my firstborn daughter, I wondered how God would meet me in the raw questions stirring inside of me. How would He continue to write hope on my heart?

It was hard to comprehend, in the midst of such agonizing loss, that the life and death of my first and then second daughter would lead to knowing the hope that doesn't disappoint. In fact, I could not have known then that as I learned to wrestle with God, my heart would become more settled in the mystery, more surrendered to Him as the author of the greatest story ever told—a story in which I have the privilege of playing just a small part.

This is my story of how the hope that doesn't disappoint was forged in my heart and how my companions of Sorrow and Suffering were being transformed into Joy and Peace. And it's a story of how, when death invaded my life, life invaded it more.

It is not a linear journey where pretty bows are tied along the way. Far from it. It's a journey of deep soul wrestling, of the constant mingling of joy and sorrow. It's a journey where often I thought I was moving backward instead of forward. A journey where God's grace has been sufficient for me as He has lifted my eyes above the sadness and heartache to give me small glimpses of His hand at work, writing hope and joy into the sad pages of our story. And it's a journey of discovering there is no amount of wavering faith that can undo the unwavering faithfulness of God in my life.

Oh, how I hope you would discover this God in your own journey too. That you would discover the rich intimacy and love of the One who writes the kind of hope that doesn't disappoint into our hearts in the midst of our disappointment. It isn't often written on the mountaintops, or seasons of ease. But it is written in the very darkness where mist surrounds, His truths shrouded in mystery, and we cannot see what is ahead. These are the unexpected places hope has been forged more deeply in my heart. And I pray you would discover how these are the places where He is forging His hope more deeply in your heart, too, in the things you are waiting for, in your suffering, and as you surrender your story to Him.

For the days my dreams were buried in the ground were the days God was already at work bringing life into death. Of course, I couldn't see more than millisecond glimpses at the time. But they were there, and even if you cannot see it now, they are there in your story too.

Years earlier God was preparing my heart for these very chapters in my story, teaching me what true hope is and how we can be rooted in the hope of God more deeply. I thought they were just lessons for my young-adult years, but I discovered they were a deepening foundation for now.

# TWO

## THE WAITING HOPE

*If you want to fully know the goodness of God,*
*give yourself more than ever*
*to a life of waiting on him.*

—Andrew Murray

I stood on the edge of the cliff, afraid to look down. Tethered to a cord I only hoped would hold me, I moved one foot behind the other and began to rappel down the gray sandstone rock. It was 2007, and I was a single twenty-eight-year-old in the middle of the Red River Gorge in Kentucky. I had backpacked with a group of friends into the "wild," and I was a real explorer, living off the land.

Never mind that several of our friends, who organized the trip and actually had all the skills to live off the land, had told us everything we needed to bring. They cooked for us, set up our tents, and made us coffee in the morning. Meanwhile my best friend, Julie, brushed her teeth with her electric toothbrush just beyond the tents.

We were roughing it, or at least our version of "roughing." I was living the epitome of adventure, and coffee from what looked like a little tea bag tasted like the best coffee in the world.

It was fall, and the leaves had turned that kind of golden orange, red, and almost pink that made it look as if an artist had painted a masterpiece. And I had the privilege of sitting in the middle of this grand display of the splendor of my Creator.

These were scenes I had seen countless times growing up in the Midwest, but they still gripped my heart with wonder. I loved being in this place, surrounded by rocks and cliffs, trees and flowers. Squirrels scurried about, and the occasional deer would allow us to see their dance through the forest. It is unsettling how beauty and terror can collide so quickly.

I had rappelled before—OK, only once, but still I had determined I was quite good at it. This time, however, a large ledge obstructed my view to the bottom of the ravine. I wondered if there would be anyplace to put my feet against the side of the cliff as I worked my way over. Would I be dangling in thin air?

Just moments before, I was sitting several feet back, watching friend after friend hesitate on the edge. I determined I would descend quickly; there would be no hesitation.

From a distance, even a short distance, the ledge didn't look so difficult to step over. But that was when I wasn't the one on the ledge. I hadn't yet experienced what it was like to be unable to see where the wall of rock was to stabilize my feet once I had the courage to lower myself. I hadn't yet had a rope harnessed to me that I only hoped our friend had tied correctly before trusting it to hold my weight.

---

Burying our firstborn daughter was one of those devastating moments. Yet it was in the years before her birth that the hope that actually has the power to hold you fast in life's most devastating moments was beginning to be woven in my heart.

---

I was sitting on solid ground a safe enough distance from the ledge, and fear hadn't captured me yet. You can't discover if you'll survive the thing you fear until you are asked to face it.

Fear is a strange thing when you are the one on the edge. If you think too much, you can end up paralyzed, a thousand what-ifs pulverizing your mind. Well, I thought too much, and the terror gripped me. I was just like everyone who had gone before me.

After what seemed like an eternity, I took the first step over the edge. In an instant I turned upside down. My back slammed against the rock underneath the ledge that was now peering out above my feet as I stared at the bottom of the ravine. I had released the rope too quickly and flipped over the ledge.

Terrified at the sudden drop, I wondered for a moment if I was about to plunge to my death, yet the rope still held me. The clasps around my harness, designed to stop any kind of sudden fall, were functioning to perfection.

I laughed, too stunned to respond any other way, and told everyone I was OK (they'd simply seen me disappear fast over the ledge), albeit sore. I then sank into my harness and rappelled the rest of the way down with much caution. I enjoyed the experience a little more the closer I came to the bottom.

The strength of the rope tightening over the harness kept me from a free fall. And even though my terror of stepping off the ledge left me paralyzed for a moment, it didn't change the ability and strength of the rope to hold me. Once I allowed the rope to bear the weight of my body and stopped trying to bear it myself, it sustained me.

Hope is like that.

It's what we hold onto amid the uncertainties of life, the disappointment, and heartache.

Webster's dictionary defines *hope* as "to want something to happen or be true and think that it could happen or be true."

I desire a lot of things to happen or be true. That day I hoped it was true that the rope would hold me, and it did what I hoped. But there are many days when I place my hope in things that aren't true or that unfold far differently than I had hoped. Sometimes the results of placing my hope in something that doesn't end up happening seem to be inconsequential, and other times the results are devastating.

It is in those times of devastation that I have had to evaluate where my hope really is. Is there a hope that can hold me when I'm on the edge of a cliff about to plunge to my certain death?

Burying our firstborn daughter was one of those devastating moments. Yet it was in the years before her birth that the hope that actually has the power to hold you fast in life's most devastating moments was beginning to be woven in my heart.

⁂

Just a few months after clinging upside down to that rope on the edge of the cliff, I walked on cobblestone roads, passed buildings that held thousands of years of history, and entered an old church in Rome. I was meeting with a team of missionaries I was working with for the week. We opened our Bibles to Isaiah 25:9 as Sam, one of our leaders, walked us through a quick Bible study to prepare us for the week ahead.

"How does our Western culture view waiting?" Sam asked. We all threw out our thoughts.

"Time-oriented."

"Event-driven."

"Sequential."

"How do I get from point A to point Z the quickest way possible?"

Or better put, "How do I spend the least amount of time waiting?"

When I'm looking at where to stand in line at the grocery store, I choose the line I'm convinced will be the shortest. More times than not, I choose the wrong line and then get frustrated. We prefer not to wait, but there are always things we are waiting to see happen in our lives.

We read Isaiah 25:9, "Behold, this is our God for whom we have waited that He might save us." In this verse, the prophet Isaiah is speaking of the day when death is defeated, the day the Lord will wipe away our tears forever and do what He had promised long ago: redeem and restore His people and His world. And on that day the people will declare together, "Behold, this is our God for whom we have waited" (v. 9).

---

In this particular season, I often questioned God's faithfulness, His trustworthiness, and His goodness. It seems those have become the questions of nearly every season, but God was inviting me to bring my questions to Him. To actually wrestle with them.

---

I didn't catch much of the power of the words Isaiah was saying previously—death being defeated, tears wiped away, all redeemed. I hadn't yet experienced the gravitas of those words and how essential they were to our hope. My ears were attuned to the waiting part.

Of course I longed for Christ's return, for the day when all would be made new, but the most pressing matters of my heart were marriage-centered, not eternity-centered. But, oh, how I wanted God to transform my heart and use this deep desire for marriage to show me more of Himself and turn my desire toward Him.

Why is it that often when we read the Old Testament it seems as if stories are told and then retold? More details are given in some places than in others. We see a greater fluidity than in our orderly and sequential society. Eastern culture was less concerned about an event but rather about what was happening in the process of the waiting for the event. Eastern culture (and many other cultures outside of America) are much less time-oriented in the daily rhythms of life.

I experienced this when I lived in the Eastern European country of Macedonia for a year. I would often set a time to meet with someone, and they would show up an hour later. Why? Because they were still in conversation with the person they were meeting before me. What was happening in that time was more important than what came next *in* time.

The Hebrew word for "to wait" is the word *qavah*. It means "to wait, look for, hope, expect, bind together."[1] The word for waiting and hope often are interchangeable in the Old Testament. But the part that struck me in this word *qavah* as we studied it that day in Rome was being bound together. This word also refers to a cord or a rope. The binding or twisting that is happening is like a rope that grows tighter and stronger the more threads twisted through it. And the more threads woven into a cord, the more weight it can bear, keeping the cord from breaking when the tension comes.

I wondered what God's people really meant as they declared, "This is our God for whom we have waited that He might save us" (v. 9). Of course they were saying that He finally did what He said He would do—He finally saved and redeemed and restored. But there is also a deeper declaration of faith happening. They are also saying not only did God do what He said He would do, but we allowed Him to do a work in our hearts *in* the waiting. In essence as we waited, our hearts were being strengthened by a deepening understanding and conviction of who our God is.

So what is being bound together in our hearts in our waiting? What does it mean to wait well? As a single twenty-eight-year-old, my immediate thought went to waiting well for my future husband. I didn't want to stand at the end of the aisle on my wedding day and say with a slightly bitter tone, "It's about time, Lord."

I understood that what I was ultimately waiting for was not marriage, though a man in the flesh would be quite a nice addition. But I also noticed that the longings of my heart for marriage were revealing the ways my hope was placed in a circumstance and not in the One who is Lord over my circumstances.

I was only beginning to learn what it looked like to wait on God. And much like Andrew Murray describes in his book *Waiting on God*, my hope was still set on the blessing God would give instead of the Giver of the blessing Himself in my first significant lesson on waiting.

> At our first entrance into the school of waiting upon God, the heart is mainly set on the blessings which we wait for. God graciously uses our needs and desires for help to educate us for something higher than we were thinking of. We were seeking gifts; He, the Giver, longs to give Himself and to satisfy the soul with His goodness. It is just for this reason that He often withholds the gifts, and that the time of waiting is made so long. He is constantly seeking to win the heart of His child for Himself. He wishes that we would not only say, when he bestows the gift, "How good is God!" but that long before it comes, and even if it never comes, we should all the time be experiencing: it is good that a man should quietly wait. "The Lord is good unto them that wait for him."[2]

It was as if God was inviting me into a deeper relationship with Him in ways only a season of waiting could cultivate. In this particular season, I often questioned God's faithfulness, His trustworthiness, and His goodness. It seems those have become the questions of nearly every season, but God was inviting me to bring my questions to Him. To actually wrestle with them.

It felt as though all my friends were getting what I wanted. Was God withholding goodness from me? I had to bring those questions to Him, open His Word, and discover what He really had to say about His goodness, His faithfulness, and His trustworthiness. And as a result, I drew near to God in this season in fresh ways. The season of waiting had ushered me into a deeper longing for the Giver of the gifts and not just the gift itself.

And when God gave me the gift I desired, there would be new seasons of waiting, new seasons of wrestling, and new seasons of learning to long for the Giver above the gift.

❈❈❈

Many years after sitting in that old church in Rome, that new season began. It was May 13, 2012, when I stood at the end of the aisle of a small white stucco church in Orlando, Florida, on an overcast and hot day, about to marry the man I never imagined would come into my life.

I tightly held my dad's hand while wearing my white lace mermaid gown. A long veil cascaded down my back, and a shorter one covered my face as we stood outside in front of the tall glass doors, waiting for the moment they would open and my dad would escort me down to the man of my dreams.

Kevin Patrick Dennis, a man of humility, kindness, and courage, not to mention tall, with dark hair and handsome features, was about to be my husband. I could hardly believe it.

This dream I waited for, longed for, and hoped would come into my life had come. But I knew, even in my love-struck heart, my new husband was not who I was ultimately waiting for.

For thirty-three years, singleness had been the gift God had given me to draw me deeper into knowing Him as my source of life and hope. I assuredly did not see it as a gift for much of those thirty-three years, but it had been a gift, for God had given me so much of Him in those years. He had shown me that He sees me amid the painful longings. In the relationships that went sour and left me broken, He had revealed how He restores and redeems the broken. In the tearful and joyful moments, He had led me to Himself over and over again. What a gift singleness had been. And on May 13, 2012, His gift would be marriage.

Kevin and I wanted our wedding to point to the One we are truly waiting for, the One who has given us marriage as a picture of our relationship with Him. So, all of the songs that were sung and Scriptures that were read that day were intended to lift our gaze upward—even the song that would be played as I walked down the aisle, "How Great Is Our God" by Chris Tomlin. Julie's husband, Danny, led all in attendance in worship to that song.

I walked in as the second line played. Yes, it was a bit dramatic. If my life could be a genre of a movie, I would most assuredly choose a musical.

---

Every unwelcome circumstance, every piercing of the heart, every disappointment brought before the Lord is forging in us the Hope that does not disappoint and pointing us to true resurrection hope. For the greatest pain in our lives exposes what we really believe about God and is fertile soil for God to do His greatest work in our lives.

---

"And time is in His hands, beginning and the end, beginning and the end," Danny sang.

Cue the doors, cue me in my lacy gown, cue the tears, cue the joy, cue my eyes fixed solely on that handsome man at the end of the aisle waiting for me, cue my heart in awe of what God had done.

Arm in arm, my dad and I slowly made our way down the aisle. The light radiated through the glass windows that covered both sides of the small church in such a way that the room had a golden aura about it. Or was that my glassy, love-filled eyes? Probably the latter; the video footage didn't quite capture the golden aura.

We chose that song to lift our eyes to the goodness and greatness of God in providing us for each other. And ultimately to be a reminder of our hope that our marriage would declare His greatness in all He asked us to step into.

That day before the doors opened and Kevin became my husband, I remembered those words in Isaiah 25:9: "Behold, this is our God for whom we have waited that He might save us," which are inscribed on the inside of Kevin's wedding band. Silently I prayed, "God, I haven't waited perfectly, but thank You that You enabled me to press into You, to strengthen my cord of hope as I waited for this next phase of my life."

And then moments later, with eyes only for my husband, we stood across from each other saying our vows.

> I promise to be faithful to you, in good times and in bad; in plenty and in want; in sickness and in health; through the pressures of the present and the uncertainties of the future. I will never leave you. I will stay with you for as long as we live on this earth, or until Jesus returns. Until that day, we will serve each other as a family and serve the world with the gospel of Jesus Christ. I make this covenant, depending not on my own strength, in which I would fail, but I commit to depend on the leading and the empowerment of the Holy Spirit, who will always prevail, as we step into this great adventure of faith ahead of us.

We had no idea in the blissfulness of that moment that months later, the hope that had been woven in our hearts over many years of trusting God would be stretched beyond all possibility. The future uncertainties we spoke of would be challenged in ways that would force us to hold true to the vows we said in innocence and ignorance that day; that God would take us on a journey of forging hope into our hearts deeper still.

The notion that our dreams for the future would come crashing down in a few short months was hardly imaginable as we sped away in a red convertible, my hair blowing in the wind, and the entire world ahead of us.

These seasons of learning to invite God into the raw places of my heart and letting Him more deeply embed the truths of His character in my life were foundational seasons for me. They were the very places where God was teaching me how to lean on Him, the Rock that is unshakable. And they are the seasons where He can weave those same truths into your life as you invite Him into your pain and allow Him to meet you there.

Every unwelcome circumstance, every piercing of the heart, every disappointment brought before the Lord is forging in us the Hope that does not disappoint and pointing us to true resurrection hope. For the greatest pain in our lives exposes what we really believe about God and is fertile soil for God to do His greatest work in our lives.

Do we believe He is good? Is He really our hope? In God's abundant grace and desire to be known rightly by us, He will be faithful to take even the most painful circumstance to draw us deeper into a right knowledge of Him. For He knows that when we know Him rightly, we will be changed. And we will know the hope that is secure and steadfast, able to hold us fast when the tension life brings feels as though we may be broken in two.

# THREE

## THE DARKNESS BEGINS

*Joys are always on their way to us,*
*they are always traveling to us*
*through the darkness of the night.*
*There is never a night when they are not coming.*

—Amy Carmichael, "Joy and Satisfaction"

It was December 2012, seven months into newlywed life, and I felt unusually tired. Like I had just run a marathon but had only walked up and down a few flights of stairs. The thought crossed my mind that perhaps I was pregnant, so out of curiosity and wanting to put my mind at ease I took a pregnancy test when I got home from work.

Kevin had a meeting with a friend and wouldn't be home until later. But of course it would be negative, so I didn't think I needed to wait for him.

I took the test and stood there by the little stick on the counter of my bathroom sink, watching one line and then two lines appear. Positive. Disbelief and shock seemed to render me immobile for a moment before it sank in.

We had just started to *try* to get pregnant. I was thirty-three, Kevin was thirty-four, and we had so many friends struggle with infertility that we assumed the journey to form our family would not be easy. So, I was standing there in front of a positive pregnancy test in disbelief at God's blessing and provision.

*Oh, how good He is to us,* I said with joy in my heart as I wondered, *Surely, He is blessing our faithfulness to Him.*

It was the seed of a view of God that He blesses us with good things (our idea of good things) based on what we do for Him. This view would be challenged in just a few short months. And yet, this was not a picture of how God worked that I would have said I believed. It's interesting how your circumstances will display what you truly believe about God's character. But in that moment, no part of me even considered that I could be off on my view of God and how He worked. All that was on my mind was *How will I tell Kevin?*

I could feel my heart beating a thousand miles a minute.

*Where is he?*

*When will he be home?*

*Can I throw together a fun way to surprise him?*

I became slightly frantic in my excitement and urgent need to see him.

---

Daily, Kevin and I would thank God for this little baby and entrust him or her to the Lord. And then we went in for my twenty-week ultrasound.

---

It was December 5, 2012, and we had just put up our five-foot Christmas tree that fit perfectly in the corner of our apartment living room. So I hurriedly found a Christmas tin to put the pregnancy test in, scribbled a poorly written riddle, and put it under our tree.

> Kevin,
> A very special Christmas gift lies underneath.
> It's coming to you early just because it is so sweet!
> We've had many memories at Disney,
> So let's just make one more,
> And start this Christmas Celebration right
> As you open up the lid.
> Love you, your wife

I put my phone on the ground to film, recording what would end up being just our feet. I had intentions of capturing Kevin's shock and joy, but did I think we would lie on the ground to open this gift? All I can remember is that excitement and disbelief were blurring all rational thought. Also, I was pregnant, so that had to be affecting my mental reasoning at some level, too, right?

I spent the next half hour pacing back and forth, looking out our window until finally he was at the door.

*Now, how to keep a straight face? God help me. I am notoriously not good at this.*

---

Oh Lord, even in this season would you
teach me Joy Unspeakable. That I would have
joy and a thankful heart with every aspect of
this pregnancy.

---

I avoided eye contact and quickly told him there was a gift he needed to open under the Christmas tree. It was something special for the night ahead since we were meeting friends at Walt Disney World. He read the riddle, which made no sense to him, opened the box, and looked with confusion at the little stick.

How did he not instantaneously recognize that two pink lines meant pregnant? I quickly filled him in. It still slowly registered as he said, "We're pregnant, we're PREGnant, we're PREGNANT," louder and louder and louder. With the screen door to our balcony open, I'm sure all of our neighbors heard as a loud guttural belly laugh of excitement rolled out of Kevin.

I picked up the phone filming our feet, and we shouted with contagious joy into the camera, "We're pregnant!" And it would become the first of many videos celebrating the life of this little baby. We came up with creative ways to tell each of our family members, and they joined in the excitement over this little life growing inside of me.

I cried, like many new mommas, when I sat at my first doctor's appointment and heard the heartbeat for the first time. With joy and wonder, we'd watch this little baby kicking and squirming around in the weeks and appointments to come on a small portable ultrasound screen.

And daily, Kevin and I would thank God for this little baby and entrust him or her to the Lord. And then we went in for my twenty-week ultrasound.

❊❊❊

The morning of March 27, 2013, was a normal, uneventful morning. I sat in a sun-faded chair in the corner of our bedroom looking out the window at the large magnolia tree that blocked much of the view of the other apartment buildings. I loved that little spot. Peaceful and serene.

Twenty weeks pregnant, my feet up and Bible in my lap, I don't remember what I read or prayed that morning.

I guess I assumed, since no words jumped out at me in those still small moments with God, that the rest of our day, including our twenty-week ultrasound, would be uneventful too. I had forgotten about what I had prayed just a week earlier. Written in my journal were words from the devotional *Streams in the Desert*, along with a prayer of mine that, looking back, would be quite providential.

---

Our lives had just turned upside down, and
all that was joyful about that day was erased
in the matter of a moment. How quickly joy
and terror collide.

---

"As sorrowful, yet always rejoicing [2 Corinthians 6:10]. Have you learned this lesson yet? Not simply to endure God's will, nor only to choose it; but to rejoice in it with joy unspeakable and full of glory."[1]

I had written in my journal a few weeks earlier:

> *Joy unspeakable.*
> *Lord, I spend so much time simply choosing*
> *to endure the lots you've given that are less*
> *than what perhaps I'd hoped for, waiting for*
> *when the next season should come in impatient*
> *anticipation. I think of pregnancy with this.*
> *The joy unspeakable of having a child, feeling*
> *this baby move . . . yet with all the discomforts,*
> *sleeplessness, a growing body, I find myself simply*
> *enduring. Oh Lord, even in this season would you*
> *teach me Joy Unspeakable. That I would have*
> *joy and a thankful heart with every aspect of this*
> *pregnancy.*

I had forgotten that prayer. Joy unspeakable. He would answer in such different ways than I expected. He often does.

⁂

Kevin and I sat in the waiting room of my OB office later that afternoon excited to see our little baby on the big screen. We'd had plenty of discussions that week of whether we'd find out the gender and decided we wanted to be surprised.

## Jesus. Jesus, we need You.
## We need You right now.

Finally called back, we were making friendly banter with the technician when she began the scan and said, "Well, I can see the sex," to which we responded in panicked unison, "Don't tell us." We all laughed.

As she continued the scan, she became increasingly silent. I wasn't concerned, until without saying a word she printed off a photo, quickly took it from the printer, and said she would be back.

A knot formed in my stomach.

The time ticked on, and Kevin and I became more and more nervous. But neither of us expressed those fears to the other so as not to make the other one nervous.

After what seemed like an eternity, she came back in with my OB beside her, who immediately sat down next to me and reached for my hand. Sadness was in our doctor's eyes. Whatever it was it wasn't good. My tears flowed as our doctor, Dr. K, who would become a dear friend, said with tenderness and deep compassion, "I'm so sorry, it's not good. We can't seem to find your baby's skull. And I want to send you right now to a high-risk doctor to take a closer look. We've already called ahead and set up an appointment."

My heart was in my throat as I tried to understand what she had said. *No skull, that sounds bad but perhaps it's not the worst, our baby is still alive.* I couldn't comprehend what she was saying.

Our lives had just turned upside down, and all that was joyful about that day was erased in the matter of a moment. How quickly joy and terror collide.

I thought nothing severe would go wrong at the twenty-week ultrasound. I was convinced the window of time to be concerned was over by twelve weeks. Of course there were rare and "random" things that could go wrong, but that happens to other people, not us. I expected it would be smooth sailing from here. I thought God was blessing us. What kind of blessing was this?

And like a scene from a slow-motion film, I got up off the chair, looked at Kevin with tears streaming down both of our cheeks, neither one of us knowing what to say to the other.

We stood in the large, sterile room, holding onto each other for dear life and spoke the words that were the only ones that found their way to our quivering lips. The only words that held the power to hold us when all our dreams had just been stripped away from us.

"Jesus. Jesus, we need You. We need You right now."

※※※

We still had no idea what kind of journey we were about to walk, but we took a deep breath and headed to our car. We prayed with an urgency that in the course of the thirty-minute drive to the next doctor, God would miraculously form the skull of our child.

We said few words to one another as Kevin drove and I sat in the passenger seat, disbelief, shock, and sadness filling the air. Kevin asked what I was thinking, and all I could say was, "What is the Lord going to ask of us?" Jesus. Jesus. Jesus. Give me courage for what may lie ahead.

We pulled into the parking lot—one we would become all too familiar with—and made our way to the second floor. It was all a blur, walking through the doors marked "Fetal Diagnostic Center," signing in, and sitting in the waiting room. Our hearts settled as we waited. This was all a dream. A higher-powered ultrasound will confirm that. The skull is there; nothing is wrong.

Robyn, our sonographer, came to get us. She was professional, kind, and to the point as she put that weird jelly on my belly. They warmed it there, and I was grateful for that. She began the scan and asked, "What are you here for?" Hope filled my heart as I thought, *She doesn't know; she must see a skull, there must be nothing wrong.*

I said, "They couldn't seem to see a skull at our OB appointment." To which she responded, "I don't disagree with that." Perhaps she wanted to know how much we knew of why we were sent there.

Crushed. God had not formed a skull in that half-hour window; maybe I was crazy for hoping He would. The bad dream was returning, only we were still awake.

Still, what did it all mean? The high-risk doctor came in, Dr. A—again, professional and kind. He explained to us the condition of our child. He said the shock of all of it would probably not enable us to remember what he had said. But we remembered every detail.

"Your baby has what's called anencephaly," he said.

*Ana-what?* I thought.

We had never heard of that before.

He continued to say, "It means that your baby's brain has not formed, and therefore his or her skull has not formed and will not."

Comprehending the devastation of this news, Kevin slowly asked: "So what does this mean?"

To which he gently responded, "There is no cure, and if you carry to term, your baby will most likely only live minutes, if that."

Minutes.

No cure.

Carry to term.

A baby can live in my womb without a brain, without a skull, but not outside. How can this be?

*Lord, give us hours*, a silent, providential prayer rose in my heart.

---

But what a joy it would be to love her for as long as God would give her to us, knowing her life would be brief, knowing our hearts would ache. It was the first moment for me where true joy and deep pain collided together.

---

"You have a few options." He said it gently and with no pressure, but my chest still tightened with anger.

I realized what he meant by "options," yet this little life on the screen, this child forming in my womb, regardless of how he or she would come into this world, was not an option. Life. We would choose life.

The doctor shared that in the state of Florida you can terminate up to twenty-four weeks of pregnancy, but I interrupted him before talking with Kevin. I knew he was thinking the same as the fierce and protective momma bear rose inside of me for the first time.

"No. We will carry our child for however long God gives him or her to us," I said with confidence and firmness.

---

Carry a child who would not live. *How can I do this, Lord?* I had no idea.

---

Dr. A gave us some space, respecting our decision and allowing this news to sink in.

After we cried and begged God for time with this little baby, I looked at Kevin with urgency in my eyes and said, "We have to find out the sex; we have to give him or her a name." We didn't know how long our child would be with us, but somehow in the midst of our great sadness we would celebrate and cherish this little baby.

Robyn came back, and I asked if we could find out the sex. She kindly put the jelly back on my belly, and I looked at the screen of our broken little baby and fell in love with this child forming in my womb all over again.

"It's a girl," Robyn pointed out with a smile on her face.

A girl. I knew it.

And now my whole body was breaking all over again. A daughter. I would have to say goodbye to my firstborn daughter.

But what a joy it would be to love her for as long as God would give her to us, knowing her life would be brief, knowing our hearts would ache.

It was the first moment for me where true joy and deep pain collided together.

Dr. A came back into the room, having set up an appointment with a genetic counselor the following morning to better understand this condition. We went through a genetic history evaluation to see if we carried any of the markers that raise flags for the chance of this condition happening. We didn't have those markers.

---

For it was in those moments of crushing pain where God was revealing that He was with us. He would walk us through this journey, and He would use His people to help us carry the tremendous weight of this pain. He did not intend us to bear it alone.

---

There is little research done on anencephaly, with very few things linked to its occurrence. It falls under the umbrella of neural tube defects, happening in three in ten thousand pregnancies.[2] However, most of those pregnancies end up miscarrying early on. And of those that don't, a majority of women who face this diagnosis terminate their pregnancy.[3] It's not necessarily because they all want to but because many have not heard of the hope that can rise from choosing to carry a child who will die or that it is even possible to carry to term. And sadly, many are told that termination is just what you do in situations like ours.

❁❁❁

When we left the doctor's office that day, it was like the air had just been taken out of our lungs. The weight of what we were about to step into seemed to be an impossible burden to bear.

Carry a child who would not live. How can I do this, Lord? I had no idea.

Kevin and I didn't know what to do. We didn't want to go home; somehow that made the news all too real, too difficult, and too painful. Yet, we didn't know how to process this together beyond our tears and needed to tell our family, but we also realized we needed community. We needed our closest friends and could not bear this burden alone.

"Do the next thing."[4] Elisabeth Elliot's words were a reflection of my heart.

The next thing that day was to go collapse in the arms of my best friend, Julie. We had laughed through much of our young-adult years together. I made fun of her for taking her electric toothbrush camping and keeping tags on all her clothes for an indefinite period of time—just in case. We celebrated each other's successes, moved to new cities together, cried over broken relationships, and stood by each other's side as we married the men who decided they'd put up with all our crazy. I celebrated the birth of her first daughter just a year and a half earlier, and she was excited to celebrate the birth of mine.

But that day we would walk through something very different together.

Julie and her husband, Danny, and their daughter, Eliana, lived just a few minutes down the street from our doctor. I had told her previously to be praying, so I quickly texted her: "Can we come over? It's not good."

Kevin and I sat in silence on the short drive to her house. We walked up to Julie's house and knocked on the door. As soon as she opened the door, it was as if the reality of what just happened hit again as we were forced to voice the words we had yet to speak aloud.

"She's not going to live," I wailed as a woman in deep grief, Kevin and I both melting now into her arms. Tears streamed down Julie's face as we began to share with her all we understood about our daughter's condition. We prayed, cried, and called our family, who prayed and cried with us. And then Danny came home, and the tears poured out all over again as we held each other, prayed, and cried more.

These moments with our best friends and on the phone with our family and other close friends were brutal and yet beautiful all at once. It was a dramatic collision of beauty and pain in the midst of community, one where hope was beginning to rise as we invited others into this new journey. For it was in those moments of crushing pain where God was revealing that He was with us. He would walk us through this journey, and He would use His people to help us carry the tremendous weight of this pain. He did not intend us to bear it alone.

⊗⊗⊗

The following day, though my eyes were swollen from tears and my body and mind weary from shock, I put together an email to send to our friends to let them into the news of our daughter's condition.

> Kevin and I are both in great sorrow and mourning over this news. Yet we trust in our great God and His goodness as we walk with Him through this. Last night we both slept very little, my mind filled with thoughts and sadness of what is to come. I want to celebrate our sweet daughter's life in the short time we have with her, but I wonder how in the world God will walk us through the intense grief of knowing we will have her for such a short time and be planning our daughter's funeral as we celebrate her arrival.
>
> I have many questions for the Lord, yet I am resting and clinging to His goodness (though times of anger may come). We are convinced that God will be greatly glorified through our daughter's short life. And we want to step into grief and this season with the hope of heaven and how God will use our story to touch the lives of many around us and through us.

We asked that others would pray for supernatural healing of our daughter's brain and skull. But in the same breath, we reminded our friends (and us) that our hope was not in a miracle, but in our God. Truthfully, Kevin was more ready to pray this than I was. I didn't want to face the disappointment of how I may respond if I prayed for healing and God didn't heal, what would that do to my faith?

I couldn't go to those places of doubt and fear then. But in the following weeks, God would take me there, and I would wrestle with His character and how He works in fresh ways.

---

I didn't wish this story on anyone else, but I couldn't help wondering why God would ask this of us. How could this piece of our story be a part of a greater story being told?

---

We asked that people would pray that God would give us days with her if He did not heal her. And that God would give me strength, hope, and joy in carrying this precious baby to full term in the midst of knowing what was coming. And we prayed that we would grieve well as a couple and in our community. There were so many prayers God began to answer yes to, and still some of the ones we longed for most got an answer of no.

My letter concluded with hope as my eyes turned to Jesus, writing:

One thing that gives us such hope is that our little daughter's first sight may be Jesus. She will never be bound by sin, and the only home she will ever know will be His and how sweet that she will be totally whole in Heaven and we will one day spend eternity with her. This season without her will seem so long, but it is so short in perspective of eternity. I laugh when I think of what her perspective will be when I see her again and she's able to communicate "Oh sweet parents, I got the best end of the deal . . . I got to be with Jesus my whole life."

But I cannot comprehend that perspective fully through my tears. Because right now I wish she would be ours for longer than a moment, and then I am reminded that she was never ours to begin with. Kevin and I have given her to the Lord so many times in our prayers. She belongs to Him, and the Lord truly is a gift giver in giving her to us, to care for in my womb and for the short time we will have with her.

We are so thankful for our family, friends, and even strangers that are praying with us for our little girl. We wish that our story for our first baby, our first daughter, would be different. But as I've learned in waiting on the Lord for many things (especially Kevin), His story for our lives is always better, always sweeter, always worth whatever suffering He asks us to go through. We hope and know we will see glimpses of those "better, sweeter, worth it" moments throughout this season. But we also know our God will use this in ways we will never get to see this side of Heaven.

"Your eyes saw my unformed substance; in your book were written, every one of them, the days that were formed for me, when as yet there was none of them" (Psalm 139:16 ESV). He knew, He knows.

With Love,
Lindsey & Kevin

The confident belief that God was at work as I wrote was intermingled with such doubt and questions almost in the same breath.

*But must it be this way? Why us?*

Of course I didn't wish this story on anyone else, but I couldn't help wondering why God would ask this of us.

How could this piece of our story be a part of a greater story being told?

Could it?

And as I brought my questions to the Lord, even in the darkness of those early weeks of our new journey, He led me to fresh surrender and deeper joy—joy woven in the darkness.

# FOUR

## THE RESISTANT HEART

*From subtle love of softening things,*
*From easy choices, weakenings,*
*(Not thus are spirits fortified,*
*Not this way went the Crucified,)*
*From all that dims Thy Calvary,*
*O Lamb of God, deliver me.*

—Amy Carmichael, "Make Me Thy Fuel"

My birthday was two days after we received our daughter's diagnosis. I didn't want to celebrate it or do anything, but we had planned to go to the beach where the rolling waves, soft sand, and ocean breeze consistently renewed and refreshed my spirit. Kevin thought it might be good for both of us to still go. I complied, begrudgingly.

I'm glad I did, for there was something about the warm ocean breeze, the sand on my feet, and a few close friends that did indeed bring refreshment and renewal to my soul—even amid the growing weight of the coming losses bearing down upon me. And for a few hours, my heart was at rest by the sea. My husband knows me well, and I'm glad he pushed back on my resistant heart.

My friend Sarah took photos of us on the beach, the first of so many memories we vigilantly keep track of. I love these photos because they captured so much of the emotion of those first few days. You can see the ache in my eyes as I hold my hand on my belly looking out at the sea before me. And you can see peacefulness in the midst of the ache as Kevin and I look into each other's eyes. This juxtaposition of ache and peace, joy and sorrow, and the back and forth of my heart as I wrestled with God's ways was so evident throughout the day.

---

> My faith displayed with such strength the day before would so quickly look like it was sitting on sinking sand. As I look back, I am brutally aware and grateful in those moments that my faith was not held by me.

---

Writing had a way of helping me sift through the madness of my mind and cling to truth in the midst of the chaos of my emotions. I wrote in my journal that day a prayer reminding me of the Hope of Christ as I reflected on spending my birthday with my daughter for the first time and also my last.

> *Today I celebrate thirty-four years of life. Thirty-four years of breath You have given me. It is a sweet and sorrowful day as Kevin and I mourn the reality that our little baby girl will most likely not have life for more than a few moments after she is born. And You are sovereign in this pain. In all the moments You've given Kevin and me over the last twenty weeks of pregnancy . . . You have been so kind. The joy of when we*

> *first found out and the opportunities to trust*
> *You in the uncertainties of the first trimester.*
> *Little untainted joys like attending a parenting*
> *conference and registering for baby things a week*
> *before we found out our little girl's condition. And*
> *now walking through the grief in knowing our*
> *child may not survive this life.*
>
> *Our world has turned upside down. And You*
> *have wrapped us in Your arms of love with such*
> *tenderness over the last couple of days. I would*
> *give anything to press rewind and hear a clear*
> *report of our daughter's ultrasound. It seems*
> *like March 27th was weeks ago, the amount of*
> *change that has occurred in the hopes and expec-*
> *tations for our future as parents.*
>
> *Oh Lord, my brain, my thoughts are dry*
> *with emotional fatigue. I know new waves of*
> *tears are just around the corner; even so, I know*
> *You see this pain. I know the One whose hand*
> *formed my daughter. The One who knew the*
> *effects of the brokenness of this world would*
> *affect our beautiful baby girl. And I know the*
> *One who holds her life together now. I know*
> *the One who can turn the brokenness of this*
> *world into sweet redemption. I know the One*
> *who makes all things new. I know the One who*
> *restores, redeems, and heals. And I know the One*
> *whose face my daughter may see before I ever get*
> *to. I know the One who holds all things together.*

Daily, I fought to believe and walk in these truths I would write with such conviction. I was telling myself like David in the psalm, "Put your hope in God, for I will yet praise Him" (43:5 NIV). Some days it was less of a fight and more of a weary resolve, while other days, other moments, even the resolve faded away.

How could I question the depth and width of
His goodness and love? Yet I questioned it. I
wondered in the finiteness of my mind how
this was His goodness and love to us?

Each morning I would wake up, pull my tired and growing body out
of bed, and make my way to the kitchen to start my breakfast. It would be
in the kitchen, as my mind would clear for the day ahead, where reality
would hit, and so would a surge of unbridled pain. In these moments every
morning, I would often say, "I don't want to go this way."

Kevin would walk in, our eyes would lock, and I would bury my head
into his chest, realizing once again: "It's all real. We will lose our baby. I
don't want this story." My faith displayed with such strength the day before
would so quickly look like it was sitting on sinking sand. As I look back,
I am brutally aware and grateful in those moments that my faith was not
held by me.

❋❋❋

The day after my birthday was Easter. It came early that year. The
day we celebrate the resurrection of our Savior Jesus who defeated death
once and for all. The day that magnifies everything the word *hope* envel-
ops. Hope beyond the grave, hope beyond our buried dreams; hope that
rises when all seems lost. And not just an arbitrary, theoretical hope, but
also the hope that lives in the person of Jesus Christ. *The* Hope that is *The*
Anchor for our soul.

Romans 8:11 says that "if the Spirit of Him who raised Jesus from the
dead dwells in you, He who raised Christ Jesus from the dead will also give
life to your mortal bodies through His Spirit who dwells in you."

Easter had never held such power as it did this time. For I needed to
not only grasp the hope of the death and resurrection of my Savior more

43

fully, but also the reality that His resurrection power could still give life to these broken places of my heart. I sat alongside the five hundred men and women in the sanctuary of our church the morning of Easter. And I was overwhelmed by the goodness of God to send His only Son to die on the cross, the worst suffering imaginable, so I could have life.

How could I question the depth and width of His goodness and love?

Yet I questioned it. I wondered in the finiteness of my mind how this was His goodness and love to us?

Intellectually I understood that in some strange way extending far beyond the wisdom of man, this was in fact His goodness and love to us. But I didn't for the life of me understand it. I desperately wanted to wrap my mind around the goodness of God shrouded now in so much mystery to me.

❊❊❊

Later in the afternoon, I was reading the story of the resurrection in the Book of John. My eyes caught a passage I had highlighted, who knows when, on the other side of the page. The words "and carry you where you do not want to go" were underlined (John 21:18 ESV).

"Do not want to go."

Yes, this was me. Every. Single. Day.

"I don't want to go this way; I don't want this to be my story" was the agonizing cry of my heart to the Lord, to myself, to Kevin, to the wall, to the wind. I needed to read this story.

In this passage, John 21, Jesus has risen from the dead and was appearing to His disciples. I'm confident His appearance was overwhelming and I'm sure a little confusing and terrifying. They had just seen Him die the most horrific death a man could die, and here He was standing before them.

Jesus knew the whole story. He always knows the whole story. He knew my whole story. And He knows yours. And in His grace, He weaves the pieces of our often confusing and broken stories into the greatest story ever told.

Jesus is with Peter and His other disciples, finishing what would be their last and final meal together, when He turns to Peter and asks, "Simeon [another name for Peter], son of John, do you love me more than these?" (v. 15). Peter, who no doubt was still reeling in shame and disappointment that at His Savior's greatest hour of need, he had denied Jesus not once, not twice, but three times just days earlier. He was now about to be asked three times from his resurrected Savior of His love for him. As Peter responds each time, "Yes, Lord; you know that I love you" (v. 15), Jesus proceeds to tell him to "Feed my lambs" (v. 15). It is only after the third time Jesus proceeds to tell him the following:

> "Truly, truly, I say to you, when you were young, you used to dress yourself and walk wherever you wanted, but when you are old, you will stretch out your hands, and another will dress you and carry you where you do not want to go. (This he said to show by what kind of death he was to glorify God.) And after saying this he said to him, 'Follow me.'" (John 21:18-19 ESV)

Wait. What? Peter just told You three times he loves You, and this is what he has to look forward to? To learn he will die in the same way as his Savior. After Jesus told him this, Peter immediately looked to the disciple sitting next to Jesus and said, "Lord, what about this man?" (v. 21). Wouldn't that be your next question?

I wondered what was going through Peter's mind. I had no idea, but I was reeling from what was going through mine. *What about them? What about women who get to walk through healthy pregnancies?* Just like Peter, I was trying to make sense of what God had just asked of me, immediately wanting to point my finger at those around me too.

But it's the words of Jesus that followed Peter's last question that stung my heart. "If it is my will that he remain until I come, what is that to you? You follow me!" (v. 22).

---

My sorrow paled compared to what Jesus went through, and countless others before me. My faith did not feel very strong, but the object of my faith was the definition of strength. I knew He was good, I knew He was worth my life and worth following even through the darkest valley.

---

You follow me.

The words echoed off the walls of my pain and confusion.

It didn't matter what His story was for others, we must follow Him. I must follow Him. My call was to follow Jesus. Jesus was not asking Peter to want to step into the pain that would come, but to follow Him in whatever He asked of him. It was not the "want to" but the willingness "to do" all God asked of him.

I didn't want to walk this path, and I was quite sure I wouldn't ever want to. But I did want to follow Jesus in it and through it.

❋❋❋

I was aware that the life of someone who followed Jesus was not a joyride. But it was a life filled with joy—the deep kind that doesn't always show on your face but erupts in your heart and through your tears. It wouldn't be a life full of ease, but would be a life full of hope—even when hope at times appeared far away. I was reminded of countless stories of

God leading His people to places they did not want to go and could not begin to understand. And each story continually resulted in greater glory, and an unfolding and unseen-at-the-time plan of redemption. Jesus knew the whole story. He always knows the whole story. He knew my whole story. And He knows yours.

---

It was in this surrender where God was inviting me to a deeper understanding of Him in ways my resistant heart would not allow. My resistance often kept my back turned toward God instead of bringing my pain to Him.

---

And in His grace, He weaves the pieces of our often confusing and broken stories into the greatest story ever told. Could Abraham have understood when God called him out into the unknown the full extent of God's promise to him to be a blessing to the nations and how God's promise would be revealed? How he would become a patriarch of the faith and a part of the lineage of Christ?

Could Job have known his faithfulness to God in the midst of the most intense pain and acute losses was a part of a cosmic war battling in the heavens? Could he have possibly seen how his honest wrestling with God would bring comfort and hope to believers for generations to come?

Could Rahab have known her small act of faith, to provide a place of safety for God's people, would not only spare her and her family's life? And that the red cord she was instructed to hang from her window, literally meaning hope, would point to the One to come who would save the world. And she, too, would be a part of the lineage of Christ.

I could go on and on of the faithfulness of God's people to trust Him even when they did not understand the whole picture. There are so many examples. Hebrews 11 is chock full of those stories. In fact, stop reading now and go read Hebrews 11.

And we also do not understand how God is taking the chapters and pages of our stories and weaving them into His grand story of redemption, glory, and hope for the nations.

Only one man lived His life knowing the whole story. Jesus. And even Jesus, right before He was to die, in the agony of knowing what would unfold, asked the Father to take this cup from Him. And still He declared, "Yet not my will but yours" (Luke 22:42 NIV). Paul sheds light on these words in Hebrews when he says, "for the joy set before him (Jesus) endured the cross, despising the shame and has sat down at the right hand of the throne of God" (Hebrews 12:2). Jesus could see the whole story. He saw the greater joy that would come from deep sorrow, and He submitted Himself to the Father's plan. He not only knew the hope, He was the HOPE.

My sorrow paled compared to what Jesus went through, and countless others before me. My faith did not feel very strong, but the object of my faith was the definition of strength. I knew He was good, I knew He was worth my life and worth following even through the darkest valley.

It was not my faith that strengthened me; it was the One who held all strength and power. I simply believed when He said, "He gives power to the faint, and to him who has no might he increases strength" (Isaiah 40:29 ESV). He would do just that. I had no idea how Jesus would do it, but somehow I was confident He would. Perhaps this is a part of how His resurrection power is at work in our mortal bodies.

> Have you not known, Have you not heard? The LORD is the everlasting God, the Creator of the ends of the earth. He does not faint or grow weary; his understanding is unsearchable. He gives power to the faint, and to him who has no might he increases strength. Even youths shall faint and be weary, and young men shall fall exhausted; but they who wait for the LORD shall renew their strength; they shall mount up with wings like eagles; they shall run and not be weary; they shall walk and not faint. (Isaiah 40:28-31 ESV)

So, as the days and weeks passed and I would daily rise and through tears say, "I don't want to go this way," I heard His still, small voice say, "Follow Me." And in my weakness I began to say so softly and timidly, "Lord, help me follow You through the places and to the places I do not want to go." My resistant heart was melting to reveal a quiet resolve and willingness to go where God called, whether I wanted to or not.

❈❈❈

It was in this surrender where God was inviting me to a deeper understanding of Him in ways my resistant heart would not allow. My resistance often kept my back turned toward God instead of bringing my pain to Him. And it was in opening my clenched fists, releasing what I could not control to His power and ways, that I was able to receive what He had to give in the midst of the pain. And He had so much to give.

It would be a daily releasing, a daily unclenching of my fists, and a growing daily awareness of what, in fact, my fingers were clenched around. It began as a releasing of my idea for my story and grew to include a releasing of my idea of who God was and how He works. Each time I released my pain to Him, I saw God meet me in the rawness.

One of those ways Kevin and I began to see His answer of help and His answer of power and strength came through the power and strength in His people. As men and women rallied around us, they lifted our arms when we had no strength and helped us celebrate the life of our little daughter. And they were a constant reminder of the hope that is ours when it appeared like hope was slipping.

As we waited for our daughter to arrive, the sorrow grew, but so did the joy as God invited others to be His vehicle of life in the midst of impending death.

# FIVE

## The Invitation

From the moment we found out a little life was growing inside of me until week nineteen, we had taken the obligatory weekly photos of my growing baby bump with our own little creative twist.

"Fifteen weeks and our sweet orange."

"Nineteen weeks and our little mango who's ready to do the tango."

That seemed so insignificant now. I didn't want to celebrate my growing belly, but the child inside my growing belly.

So we took a new picture that week after celebrating Easter at Julie's house, this time amid the pain but with a spirit of celebration growing in our hearts.

"Celebrating twenty weeks with our baby girl," our new sign and new baby bump photo declared.

Easter week could not have been a more fitting week to start a different kind of celebration. The death and resurrection of Christ was a different kind of celebration, where death turns into life. And so Easter week would be a new beginning for us, where the death of our dream for how our pregnancy and our family would develop began to give way to a new kind of life.

This period became an invitation to discover what God had for us in this new season of waiting and an invitation to press into the pain our deep disappointment brought to the surface. And it was an invitation to share in Christ's sufferings and more fully discover His joy. Our buried dreams always hold an invitation.

❁❁❁

Later that evening on our first day documenting our new celebrations, I remember talking with one of my friends, Jennafer. She tenderly asked, "What do you want to do in your time with your little girl?"

"We just want to celebrate her. We want her to meet Disney princesses and do special things with her we won't get to do with her in this life." It was a simple and subtle offering from Jennafer to be a part of our celebrations and our even more subtle invitation to let her.

I should have known *simple* and *celebration* would be two words that Jennafer had never merged. I had known her for a couple of years and I had watched her celebrate and love people with a depth I had rarely seen before. The magnitude of celebrations that would follow from that simple invitation would lead to our discovering other friends like Jennafer—friends who, without concern for themselves, would traverse the darkness with us. They became beacons of light and holders of hope for Kevin and me in ways we didn't even know we needed.

And it would be an invitation to us from God Himself to allow the body of Christ to surround us in our pain when it would be easier to just be alone—a demonstration to us and those who journeyed with us of the extravagance of His great love.

❁❁❁

A few days later, a day before I would be twenty-one weeks pregnant, Kevin took me on one of his many creative dates. He would take card games and turn them into a "choose your own adventure" type evening. He would add fun trivia to a movie night, or even take a simple dinner at home and devise a romantic evening with his own creative touches. *Dates* and *simple* were two words that didn't go together in his vocabulary. In fact, he probably should write a book on all of his extravagant dates.

---

Kevin and I were realizing we would not have to walk this journey alone, knowing how loved and celebrated our daughter was by so many already.

---

One would think his creativity would have waxed and waned as he won the girl, everyday life hit, and then tragedy hit. But no, even amid great sadness, fatigue, and the anticipation of loss, my husband's creativity and constant pursuit of my heart never waxed or waned. He wasn't perfect, of course, but he was steadfast, and I needed his steadfastness. I needed his constant pursuit of joy during this season of sorrow, even when the last thing I wanted to do was go out for an evening of fun.

That night was the first of many celebrating another week of life with our little girl. Kevin pulled out a book of names to start thinking about. And we dreamt of what we'd like our celebrations with her to look like.

Kevin had created a simple and yet beautiful piece of stationery that he meticulously titled "Timeless Treasures" with lots of swirls—not his usual style of writing, mind you. Together we started to fill that piece of paper with the memories we wanted to have with our little girl in the short time God would give us with her. Our list began quite small.

- Read the *Jesus Storybook Bible* to her.
- Take her on a daddy-daughter date.

- Take her to Magic Kingdom:
    1. Meet Mickey Mouse.
    2. Meet the princesses.
- Write her a letter.
- Take her on a mystery ride.

We stopped with just a few ideas that night, unknowingly leaving room for all the ways others would fill in the gap.

The day after our Timeless Treasure–writing, name-dreaming date, Kevin came home from a meeting with some friends from church with a basket full of goodies. We were entering into our twenty-first week of pregnancy with our little girl and our second week of our new tradition of celebration.

The basket overflowed with sparkling cider, root beer, twenty-one chocolate hugs and kisses, twenty-one root beer cupcakes, and sweet notes from Jennafer, her husband, Brady, and several other friends—a twenty-first celebration fit for a baby and a pregnant mommy.

I had a hunch that the root beer resulted from my offhand comment to Jennafer the week before that I wanted to let our little girl taste a few drops of wine for her twenty-first week. Jennafer had looked at me with horror on her face, as though she really believed I would do that. I promised her I was joking, but still I imagine her skepticism led her to include the root beer to steer me off my "wayward" path.

---

Our beautiful, victorious Sophia Kyla (whom we would call Sophie). We would watch as her life reflected the wisdom of God in ways we had never seen.

---

Laughter erupted in our home that night, along with the release of so much tension. Kevin and I realized we would not have to walk this journey alone, knowing how loved and celebrated our daughter was by so many.

It made little sense, the eruption of laughter, even the feeling of joy mingled with so much sadness. And yet our little girl already reflected to us in her broken state the reality of the words of Isaiah when he spoke of the Savior to come. This Savior would give "The oil of gladness instead of mourning, The mantle of praise instead of a spirit of fainting" (Isaiah 61:3). And God was bringing gladness where, in the wisdom of man, there should not have been gladness and praise where there should not have been praise. So as our twenty-second week approached, we realized she needed a name that held the weight of what her story and life already revealed.

❈❈❈

Paul's words to the Corinthians: "God chose the foolish things of the world to shame the wise" (1 Corinthians 1:27 NIV), reminded us of our daughter, her new journey and ours.

In the eyes of the world our daughter was weak, insignificant, had little to no value, and certainly wasn't esteemed enough to have a life simply because of her condition. For many, it didn't make sense that we would carry a child that would not live. But we understood the "foolishness of God is wiser than human wisdom" (1 Corinthians 1:25 NIV).

God's wisdom is not like ours.

It rarely makes sense why God does what He does. Yet we trusted that God was penning a story for our little girl and us that perhaps would never make sense this side of heaven, but one day the veil would lift and we would see in full. Like Paul says, "Now I know in part; then I shall know fully" (1 Corinthians 13:12 NIV).

Would He choose to use this weak and broken little girl to show those watching His power, might, and love?

The Greek name for wisdom is "Sophia," and Kevin and I couldn't shake this idea of her life being about the wisdom of God and not the wisdom of man. So at twenty-two weeks in the womb, this little girl had a name.

Sophia Kyla Dennis.

Kyla, Gaelic to honor Kevin's Irish heritage, means "beautiful." Our daughter's beauty lay not in how she looked, but because of who she was—an image-bearer of God, His daughter and ours. We soon discovered that Kyla also meant "victorious" in Hebrew, and what a victory she would soon experience! Not the victory I wanted for her so quickly out of the womb, but the victory we are all longing for when death no longer has hold of us and we are set free from this body of sin.

Our beautiful, victorious Sophia Kyla (whom we would call Sophie). We would watch as her life reflected the wisdom of God in ways we had never seen.

I decided that the most fitting way to celebrate our daughter having a name would be to make her first cake. Growing up, for our birthdays, my mom would ask us what kind of cake we wanted. Most often we would ask for her delicious ice-cream cakes: homemade with our favorite flavor of cake and our ice cream of choice between the layers. These were small and yet sweet traditions I had dreamed of having with our children. Plus, I loved ice-cream cakes. Who doesn't?

For Sophie's name reveal, I made a chocolate cake, cut into four layers with rich and decadent spreads of black raspberry chip ice cream between them, topped with whipped-cream icing. The words "Happy 22 weeks Sophia Kyla" were written in unprofessional pink script. I covered the top with little yellow flowers. It was every bit as delicious as it sounds.

My in-laws sent us twenty-two pink, yellow, and white carnations. And Kevin's best friends, Craig and Bryn, and their children came to visit all dressed up in hipster clothes in honor of Taylor Swift's new and timely "22" song. I happily put headphones up to my belly throughout the week so Sophie could dance along to the song I was sure had been written just for her.

Another friend from church, Sarah, asked if she could come over that week. She showed up at our door with a beautiful pink box filled with all the supplies we would need to have our first tea party with Sophie— from teacups, a hat, and pink boa. I remember how amazed I was that on the previous Thursday and on that Thursday someone had just shown up to help us celebrate the life of our little girl. What were the chances?

Well, there was the fact that Jennafer (who, again, had never merged the words *simple* and *celebration*) had created a secret Facebook group titled "We love Sophia Kyla" that now had more than one hundred members. So the chances were high that the weeks that followed would contain a vast array of surprises. But I didn't know about this group until well after Sophie came into the world.

❖❖❖

Amid the joy of celebrating Sophie, I would plunge into deep sadness. The realities of what was coming and the fear of how I would face what was ahead felt insurmountable. These moments of celebration brought reprieve and joy and allowed the weight to lift, if only for a few moments, hours, or days.

> God was teaching us that to fight this battle we needed others. We needed people to help us walk with Him, and we needed their strength to lift us up when ours was failing.

A week later, week twenty-three, we received a package in the mail from two women, Mo and Crista. They had been in a Bible study I had led many years earlier. They had themed our twenty-third week with Sophie and included the following note:

> *This week is STAR week! Take Sophia Kyla to the beach where you were engaged (or any open space outside) on a clear night and point out the constellations with the included map. We have also included a "Magic Carpet" you can sit on*

> *as you look up at the stars. There is some coffee (for Kevin) and tea (for Lindsey) to signify the morning and night. Read Psalm 8:3-5 to Sophia. "When I look at your heavens, the work of your fingers, the moon and the stars, which you have set in place, what is man that you are mindful of him, and the son of man that you care for him? Yet you have made him a little lower than the heavenly beings and crowned him with glory and honor." [ESV]*

In the package was a certificate and map of where a star was registered in Sophie's name. Mo and Crista wrote, "We pray that this will be a continual reminder as you gaze into the starry night that just as our Father knows all the stars in heaven by name, He watches over and cares for you, and holds Sophia safely in His hands."

---

Our suffering always carries with it an invitation to joy, an invitation to know with greater depth the happily ever after we truly long for. For how can we long for God's Kingdom when we are living easy, comfortable lives, unable to see the true brokenness in our little kingdom?

---

I continued to be amazed and perplexed as to how people knew we would celebrate "Sophie's weekly birthdays" (Can you call them birthdays? Well, we did.) on Thursdays. It wasn't until the next Sunday when we were talking with Renaut's wife, Brooke, about how we were doing and sharing with her about the ways we had been celebrating Sophie's life that the perplexing pieces came together.

Brooke casually mentioned in our conversation, "Oh, I wanted to sign up for this coming week, but we had to wait until a later week."

*Signups?* I didn't say that out loud, but I had no idea what she was talking about.

I smiled and enthusiastically responded with something like, "Oh, that is great!" pretending like I knew.

Turning to Kevin after we left, I said, "Do you think someone is organizing helping us celebrate each week?"

He had just assumed I had figured out what must be happening, but I certainly had not. I thought God was orchestrating events and prompting people to help us. I did not believe we would have a celebration every week aided by another. Nor did I even expect it, even after knowing that seemed to be the case. Kevin and I simply enjoyed how God was choosing to provide for us in this season of pain. And we welcomed those who entered the joy and pain with us with great thankfulness.

※※※

This season reminded me of the story of Moses in the Book of Exodus as the Israelites were fighting the Amaleks. God had told Moses that as long as his staff was lifted high, the Israelites would be winning, but when his arms dropped, they would lose. But Moses was human and could only lift his arms for so long. So his brother, Aaron, and another man would lift Moses's arms when he grew tired, and the people of God would continue to win. (See Exodus 17:8-16.)

God was teaching us that to fight this battle we needed others. We needed people to help us walk with Him, and we needed their strength to lift us up when ours was failing. God would be our source of strength, but He would use His strength in His people to continue to fuel that strength in us. Others would hold this hope that was ours as a beacon of light so that in moments of deep despair and discouragement, we were never far away from the truth being waved in front of us.

This is what Jennafer did for us as she rallied others to come alongside us. Perhaps she didn't even realize it. The gathering of people to help us celebrate Sophie each week became less about the celebrations, however wonderful and memory-making they were, and more about what God was doing in the celebrations. For in the celebrations, He was revealing more of Himself and more of His story through His people. We had never experienced the body of Christ functioning in such beautiful ways. Each person brought their unique gifts and abilities to our story, which lifted our eyes to God's story.

Perhaps this is the invitation in our suffering all along, an invitation into His story. And it seemed that God was writing the story for our little girl's life in such a way that not only would our lives be lifted to eternal things, but the lives of so many others would be lifted to eternal things as well.

God invited us to carry a daughter who would not live, to steward her life, and He showed us that His hope, true resurrection hope, comes out of the grave. And He invited us to welcome His people into our story. For in the waiting, the waiting to meet our first daughter, the waiting for death, the waiting for the unknown, God was teaching us that He shows up in our pain in far more different ways than we expect.

Much the same way Jesus showed up on this earth more than two thousand years ago, not as a reigning king but as a suffering Servant. Jesus would conquer death and sin through suffering, and in the darkness of the grave He would reveal hope as He rose again—the confident hope that death won't have the final say, that darkness will not last, that full redemption is coming. Our stories are small tastes of that coming redemption. We often want the invitation to be only blessing and happiness and getting our hearts desire. But God knows those things are cheap imitations of true joy and happiness. Our suffering always carries with it an invitation to joy, an invitation to know with greater depth the happily ever after we truly long for. For how can we long for God's Kingdom when we are living easy, comfortable lives, unable to see the true brokenness in our little kingdom? And how can we come to know God's heart with greater depth without being invited to wrestle with the questions suffering brings to the surface?

# SIX

## The Hope for Healing

*Healing will come, and it won't be a halfway job.*

—Joni Eareckson Tada

A crowd of people gathered in a large room. Kevin and I stood in the center. Cameras, lights, and people with microphones pressed in as if something spectacular was about to take place, but I didn't understand what. A curtain separated this large gathering from something happening outside the curtains.

"Someone has a gift for you," a woman said with a large smile.

The curtain drew back, and several people rolled in a beautiful wicker bassinet. I began to weep.

"We are trusting in God with you to heal your daughter," they said.

Could it be? Would God heal Sophie? The mere possibility of it stirred my soul to awe, wonder, and hope. The crowd pushed in on us, microphones in the hands of some as if to interview us. Whatever was about to happen would be big. But I couldn't decide whether to take the bassinet. I couldn't decide whether I could trust God to heal her, the tears flowing freely.

And then I woke up. Those same tears flowed now in reality. It had been a dream; it wasn't real. There was no bassinet in our home. There was no promise of healing. No cameras pressed in with eager anticipation of what spectacular event was about to unfold.

I have vivid dreams often, but I don't typically remember them. If I do, they are laced with all kinds of strange people, events, and weird dimensions of time and space. Rarely are they so clear.

---

I was afraid of how crushed I would be if I trusted Him to heal our daughter and He didn't. I was afraid of what that would do to my belief in God; would my faith be crushed too? Would I discover a God who isn't who I thought He was? I didn't want to go there.

---

Was God speaking to me in this dream? How do dreams work? I'm still unsure, but this dream stirred something inside of me. It exposed the deep question in my heart in the aftermath of finding out our daughter would not live. What did it mean to trust God for healing?

I remember driving to a little picturesque town in Orlando called Celebration, Florida, in the early weeks of finding out this new journey we would be on and thinking about healing. I thought about the biblical woman who was bleeding and pushed through a crowd to touch the robe of Jesus and she was healed (Luke 8:43-48). She didn't care what people thought of her; she didn't care who saw her. She just knew who held the power of healing in His very robes and stopped at nothing to be near His healing power.

---

I am confident that God, in His tenderness, wants to meet us in the dark places of our faith. He wants to build our faith there as we press into Him with our fears and questions.

---

During that drive, as I was turning left through the four lanes of traffic on a busy road onto a smaller road lined with beautiful white fences, scattered flowers, and immaculate landscape, I cried out: "Jesus, if I saw You in the middle of the road I would stop and run to You. I wouldn't care what traffic I stopped or who watched or how ridiculous I looked if I could only touch Your robe. If You would only heal my daughter."

I hoped He would heal, I believed He could, but would He? And the bigger question was: Is this the greatest prayer of my heart? For if I was honest, the moment our doctor told us our daughter would live only minutes if we were lucky, and would probably not make a sound, my immediate prayer was, "Lord, give us hours, and let us hear her cries." This was the prayer I believed He would answer. But a full healing? What does it mean to pray in faith, to pray believing God hears and wants to answer? Did God want to answer my prayer for healing?

⊠⊠⊠

A bit shaken from the dream, and still just a few weeks after finding out Sophie would not live, I told Kevin what I had seen in that dream the following morning. We wondered if God wanted us to take a step of faith to buy a bassinet, in faith, in hope, as a picture that though we knew God may not heal we believed that He could. He didn't need us to prove our faith to move, but it seemed a step of faith for us was to get a bassinet. As I researched bassinets, new stirrings in my heart arose of what I believed about God's character, His ability, and His heart. And of course, the bassinet I fell in love with was similar to the one I saw in my dream: a brown wicker Moses-type of basket with beautiful white bedding. Pottery Barn, Restoration Hardware—these were the places I found the bassinet, and they were quite out of our price range. So I looked on one of my favorite sites to browse and find all of our furniture: Craigslist.

The day that I looked online someone had posted this exact bassinet. It was beautiful, and much cheaper. It was still available that day, so Kevin was going to go pick it up. But before he left, I second-guessed whether this was a good idea, and Kevin reminded me as we talked that the steps of faith we take are often filled with wonderings and uncertainties, but the key is we still take them.

When Kevin arrived at the home, the woman, Lou Anne, whose bassinet it was, told of how her grandchildren had used it and were grown up now. Kevin proceeded to tell her our story of hope and impending loss. She was moved and amazed and cut the price in half, also giving us the blue trimmed Pottery Barn bedding to go with it "just in case" we would ever have a little boy. I was in awe and so thankful when Kevin came home and told me the story.

A week later after reading about our story on the blog I had begun to chronicle our journey, Lou Anne contacted me and said she wanted to give us the bassinet as a gift of faith with us and to send back the money we had given her. And so it was that this dream of a bassinet had become a gift from the Lord. *What did it mean?* I wondered. Could it mean we would bring home our little girl? Could it mean He would heal her? Or was God doing so much more than answering our prayers for healing but revealing more of Him in the wrestling?

❋❋❋

When we first found out our daughter's condition, the idea of praying for healing produced great fear inside of me. Was it lack of faith, or was it that God was not actually asking us to pray for healing? I think a little of both. I was afraid of how crushed I would be if I trusted Him to heal our daughter and He didn't. I was afraid of what that would do to my belief in God; would my faith be crushed too? Would I discover a God who isn't who I thought He was? I didn't want to go there.

Yet well-meaning friends challenged me to pray for her full healing. Some said I carried the responsibility to fight for her in prayer. Some said I needed more faith. Some said God's will was to heal her, that it wasn't His will to see us suffer like this. None of those comments ever sat well with me. All I remembered in God's Word was that there is never a promise for healing this side of heaven, but there is a promise of all things made new in the new heaven and the new earth (Revelation 21). There is never a promise that God doesn't want us to suffer; there is, in fact, a promise that we will suffer and He will be with us in our suffering (John 16:33; Romans 8). The healing we long for is not just freedom from disease, from death, but freedom from the effects of sin that manifests itself in our sour attitudes, addictions, broken relationships, diseases, famine—the very genetics that run through us.

If the ultimate prayer was for our little girl's physical healing, she would still die one day. Of course, we would prefer that death to be beyond even our deaths, and not the moment of or moments after her birth.

Sometimes we think, or others think, we need to just muster up this grand faith right away and discount all the emotions running through us. But as I've been on this journey, I am confident that God, in His tenderness, wants to meet us in the dark places of our faith. He wants to build our faith there as we press into Him with our fears and questions. Hebrews 11 recounts stories of men and women of faith, and I'm reminded that the majority of those men and women had faith built over time through deep encounters with God. Yet so many of them who experienced excruciating pain also never saw the redemption of their pain this side of heaven. The writer of Hebrews says, after recounting person after person who walked by faith, "And all these, though commended through their faith, did not receive what was promised, since God had provided something better for us, that apart from us they should not be made perfect" (Hebrews 11:39-40 ESV).

The promise was coming in the person of Jesus, but none of them saw Him or even knew His name. But we do. We are the "us" the writer is speaking of who can now see a bigger picture than they could. Yet we, too, still live in the between of the here and the not yet, getting tastes and glimpses of redemption while waiting in faith for the full redemption and healing that is coming.

In Matthew 17:20, Jesus says to His disciples, "For truly, I say to you, if you have faith the size of a mustard seed, you will say to this mountain, 'Move from here to there,' and it will move; and nothing will be impossible to you." Do you know that a mustard seed is incredibly tiny but when planted produces a plant that literally takes over everything? My faith felt like a mustard seed faith more often than not, and I began to realize that was enough. It's small steps of faith, taken over and over again, that inevitably grow larger and larger without you even realizing what has happened.

❊❊❊

When we had brought home the bassinet, Kevin and I put on the beautiful white bedding with two subtle pink stripes on the bumper, and the skirt. And then we knelt beside the bassinet and prayed with fervor that Sophie would get to use it. My heart grew in confidence in God's power to heal, still wondering if He would, but with a confident belief He could. Oh, how I wanted that to be His will, His plan for our first daughter's life.

Many weeks later we heard of a conference in town that focused a lot on healing. It was not a conference we would typically go to. We tend to be much more conservative in our faith, but there is something that happens when your whole world is turned upside down and when your view of God begins to be shattered and slowly rebuilt. There is something that happens when you know God says His character is one of healing and for the first time it matters more to you than ever before to know what that really means. (See Psalm 103:2-5.) When it's a matter of life and death, God as Healer becomes essential to grasp.

---

When we are in the thick of distress, it
is hard to imagine that God would come
through in ways that could be far greater
than what we even imagine praying for.

---

I was skeptical as we went to the conference and yet intrigued by how the men and women spoke of God's ability to heal and use people in that process. A man up front invited people after the session on healing prayer to be prayed for by him. We got in line and when we were just a few people away from him, he had to leave. So we did the natural thing and went back to our seats.

NO!

We ran after him.

Well, Kevin ran . . . as I was already starting to do the pregnant waddle.

For a fleeting moment I was so embarrassed that we had become these "crazy" people who would track a man down who might have the gift of healing. But I was willing to be crazy for the sake of our daughter, and so was Kevin. The man was surrounded by an entourage of his assistants, and Kevin quickly interrupted them and said with the kind of desperation a father about to lose his daughter would say, "Would you pray for our daughter?" He told them the story, and as this man walked to the next session, he placed his hand on my belly as we walked and prayed for healing.

Kevin had said, "Let's leave no stone unturned," when we decided to go to this conference.

At this point hundreds of thousands of people were praying for this little girl through word of mouth and the blog I had begun. And when we had the opportunity to be prayed for by someone who may have the gift of healing, we didn't want to have any reason to look back and say, "What if?" Later that same week, the elders at our church even gathered around us, anointing me with oil and praying for God's supernatural healing over our daughter. Leave no stone unturned.

As Sophie's arrival grew closer, I anticipated with hope and, yes, fear of what God would do. With so many praying, so many stones we had not left unturned, I knew we could not thwart His ways. I knew God would have His way with our daughter. He had heard our prayers, and He would answer. I knew it might not be the answer I wanted, but I believed it would be an answer that would reflect His goodness and glory in ways I could hardly perceive then.

The prophet Habakkuk spoke boldly God's words when he faced his own wrestling with God as he observed great oppression and devastation among God's people. "How long, O LORD?" he declared, and God answers: "Look among the nations! Observe! Be astonished! Wonder! Because I am doing something in your days—You would not believe if you were told" (Habakkuk 1:2, 5).

Even in a season of great darkness for Habakkuk and his people, God reminded him that He was at work, that He was still doing something. Something wonderful, something Habakkuk would not believe even if you had told him.

When we are in the thick of distress, it is hard to imagine that God would come through in ways that could be far greater than what we even imagine praying for. As Habakkuk prayed "How long, O LORD?" we also see our broken world, our buried dreams, our own tragedies and say the same: "How long, O Lord?" There has always been an innate longing for justice, for peace, for all the pain in this world to be eradicated, and for disease to be no more.

Yes, this is what we long for and pray for. And God reminds us through Habakkuk that He is doing something even beyond that. He will bring hope in a way that will eradicate pain once and for all, and this hope has come and will come again in the person of Jesus. Through the power of the Holy Spirit, Jesus carried the weight of the suffering and sin of the world and then destroyed its power over us in the grave, so it would not consume us.

Jesus, man of sorrows, healed physically to point to the reality that our greatest need is spiritual healing; He came to heal the greatest disease of sin upon our lives; to give us life, eternal life, a life full of meaning and purpose both here and to come. I began to believe God was going to do something so much greater than a physical healing, and that He would reveal Himself in ways we would not believe if we were told. In fact, He had been doing things we would not have believed if you had told us from the moment we found out our daughter's condition and every week after, lifting our eyes to His Kingdom and the ultimate healing we long for.

# SEVEN

## The Greatest Fairy Story

*All their life in this world and all their adventures in Narnia had only been the cover and the title page: now at last they were beginning Chapter One of the Great Story which no one on earth has read: which goes on for ever: in which every chapter is better than the one before.*

—C. S. Lewis, *The Last Battle*

K eep Thursday open" read the mysterious text we received from our friend Emily a few days before Sophie's twenty-fourth week celebration.

Thursday morning came, and another text from Emily simply said, "Meet at the entrance of the Guest Relations building at the Magic Kingdom at 2 p.m. and wear something that will go with a white T-shirt."

At twenty-four weeks pregnant, my belly had just "popped"—now looking as if a baby lived inside and not just a couple of extra pints of ice cream.

The average guest walking through the gates of Walt Disney World that day would not have had any notion that Kevin and I were taking our daughter to experience the magical world of Mickey and princesses for the first and perhaps last time. The day held weightiness mixed with a joyful expectancy of what would unfold. Every day and every celebration of Sophie's little life seemed to hold both.

Friends from our church who worked at Walt Disney World had commandeered week twenty-four to ensure that their littlest friend, Sophie, would have the most memorable day with her parents.

As we stood outside of the Guest Relations building at the front of the Magic Kingdom, Carrie, slender with long blonde hair, rounded the corner with her usual smile that can light up a room. She had a way of making you believe you've been best friends for ages.

Holding a princess gift bag in one arm, she wrapped her other arm around me and asked us both, "How are you feeling about today?"

Kevin and I both said with joy and sadness, "Excited, but not sure what to expect."

She smiled with us, knowing the weight the day held, and proceeded to say with a twinkle in her eye, "Well, we have lots of surprises for you today, but first you need to read this card and open this bag."

We opened the card, and the tears formed at once in my eyes, in Kevin's eyes, in Carrie's eyes. She had seen what was written as Kevin and I read it together:

> *Princess Sophia Kyla,*
>
> *Happy 24th week!*
> *This week you get to be celebrated like the princess you are, both because you are the daughter of the King and because you have a fairy tale of your own!*
> *We all love you so much!*
>
> *Love,*
> *Emily*

I had met Emily for the first time on the Disney Dream cruise when Kevin and I were newly engaged. Emily, Kevin, and I, along with fifteen others, were all beginning a new campus for our church that would be mainly for those who worked at Walt Disney World, called Cast Members. And it seemed only fitting that to launch this church for cast members we would go on a Disney cruise.

Many of these cast members who were helping to start the church had very close connections to some of the more popular "people" you would want to visit at Walt Disney World—people like Cinderella, Belle, Snow White, if you catch what I'm saying. I promised my Disney friends I wouldn't ruin the magic, so I can't be more specific, but I'm confident you'll figure it out. Needless to say they were quite beautiful women, and I was unusually intimidated around them at first.

I remember sitting at dinner with Emily one evening and thinking, *I hope we get to be friends.*

Emily has long brown hair, the most beautiful big brown eyes, a gentle nature, and a loving spirit, and she is rarely without some kind of adornment on her that sparkles. I couldn't believe the same girl I sat across from on that cruise had become such a dear friend and was now organizing one of the sweetest days with our daughter.

---

That day was magical. Though there were occasional tears, the joy and wonder super-seded it all. We were lifted once again by the arms of our friends to hope, joy, and celebra-tion in the thick of great darkness.

---

More surprises continued to fill the day as Kevin and I opened the gift in the bag Carrie had brought: a white shirt for Kevin with "King Kevin" printed in silver in the top left-hand corner, and a white V-neck maternity T-shirt for me that took me by surprise.

Also in silver in the top left corner was my name after "Queen." Laughter ensued when I saw that on the belly of the shirt, in large silver letters, were the words "Princess Sophia Kyla." And underneath her name, yellow sparkly mesh fabric had been ruched together with a yellow bow to make it look like a little tutu. The yellow was a nod to Princess Belle. And if you knew Emily, you'd know that she has a special fondness for Belle.

If you have ever walked down Main Street at the Magic Kingdom, stood in line to meet any of the princesses, or sat on the sidewalk as the parade goes by, you have no doubt seen countless little girls dressed as their favorite princesses. That was something, however small and trite, that I so longed to experience with my little girl. That day, as Kevin put on his shirt and I put on mine, with the little tutu gathered right at the base of my newly popped belly, I truly felt as if Sophie was putting on her little princess dress too. I'm convinced she kicked in excitement when I put it on.

The 3 p.m. "Celebrate a Dream Come True" parade was beginning soon, and a man came through the doors, dressed in a navy blue suit. He looked important.

Introducing himself, he said with a smile, "Someone special wants to meet you," and had us follow him. Carrie walked behind us after taking our camera to video what was about to unfold.

The man took us to a private waiting room, and as the doors opened, my heart jumped with giddy delight as if I was ten years old again. Right in front of me stood Belle, Ariel, the Fairy Godmother, Aurora, Snow White, and Cinderella all in a row with huge smiles on their faces.

Kevin and I went up to each of them and hugged them before they knelt down, touched my belly, and said, "Hello, Princess Sophie," as if I was not even there. It felt surreal and magical in that room. Belle looked as if she resembled my friend Emily, who had organized the day . . . or did Emily resemble Belle? Either way there was an uncanny likeness, and Belle greeted us as if she had known us for years in proper and sophisticated princess style.

The same thing happened with Snow White, who resembled my friend, Holli, though I was quite taken aback by her high-pitched voice. Aurora greeted us next, in her full pink dress, with long flowing blonde hair and a royalty about her that was a little intimidating. I couldn't quite place it, but she, too, had a familiar "aura" about her.

As each princess left the room with a final wave and "We love you, Princess Sophie," the Fairy Godmother sprinkled a little pixie dust over my belly with a twinkle in her eye. And then they were gone to catch the parade where thousands of grown men and women, little girls and little boys would be transfixed by the magic and music about to traverse the streets of the Magic Kingdom. You don't believe me? It's true. Even grown men watch with a childlike wonder. Ask my husband.

❈❈❈

Carrie hurried us out the door and down the streets of Main Street USA. We weaved in and out of the crowds already formed and ready for the parade to begin. The whole time, Kevin and I were in a state of shock, bliss, and joy that we had gotten to experience, truly experience, Sophie meeting the princesses.

That day was magical. Though there were occasional tears, the joy and wonder superseded it all. We were lifted once again by the arms of our friends to hope, joy, and celebration in the thick of great darkness.

After making our way to the front of the castle, we walked up to another man who was wearing a similar blue suit as the man earlier. He was in front of several white benches roped off and reserved for VIP guests. Carrie told him our names.

We were on the list. So he lifted the white rope that sectioned off one of the private viewing areas that Kevin and I had often walked by and wondered, "How do you get to sit in this VIP section?"

Today, we were VIPs. Or more accurately, Sophie was a VIP, and we were just along for the ride. I wouldn't have had it any other way. We sat on benches, with the castle in plain view up to our right and the music of the parade beginning just a short distance away.

The men and women holding the banner "Celebrate a Dream Come True" made their way toward us. Dancers in vibrant colors waltzed their way through the middle of the street, and one of those, to our surprise, was a good friend, Tori. As her partner swung her around, she came by our area, leaned in, and shouted, "Happy Birthday, Sophie!"

The Chipmunks were close behind. One of them came over to where the white rope was keeping us back, leaned in, pointed to my belly, and then put his hands to his face as if he were giggling with joy. *Did he know?* I wondered. I had no idea that much of the parade knew of this little girl. Already she had captured not only the hearts of our family and close friends, but those of a growing and unfolding audience, eagerly anticipating what story would unfold for Sophie.

As the music continued, evoking emotion, evoking wonder, it was as if Sophie was sitting on my lap as character after character came by acknowledging her and not us.

I laughed when the ugly stepsisters came over and in their sarcastic and off-putting way looked at my belly and said, "I wish it was a boy." The float carrying the princesses we had just met approached, and each princess waved enthusiastically. Princess Ariel shouted from afar as loud as her little mermaid voice could carry, "Happy Birthday, Sophie!"

Before the parade began, Carrie had asked me if I knew who each of the princesses resembled and I said, "I wasn't quite sure about Aurora." I thought hard, and it came to me with a little help from Carrie. She looked a little like our friend Elyse.

Elyse's friendship would unfold over the coming years in ways that would draw her into our most dark and beautiful moments and knit our hearts together forever. But today, we simply waved and yelled for Aurora with knowing eyes and smiles.

---

> For those who know Jesus, our happily ever
> after is the day when He makes all things
> new, when He welcomes us into His kingdom
> and washes away the tears from our faces. It's
> the day where death will be no more and all
> that lies ahead of us will be joy.

---

The Fairy Godmother threw what Emily would later tell me was an "obscene" amount of fairy dust over us as she rode by. As the parade came to a close with Mickey and Minnie on top of their float, Minnie noticed my belly and blew the biggest kiss, making a heart over her own belly and pointing to mine with her big white-gloved hands.

And just like that the parade was over. And our memories that day, experiencing Magic Kingdom with our little princess, would be forever etched on our minds and hearts.

It was like a fairy tale walking through the streets of the Magic Kingdom, meeting princesses, being treated like royalty, watching Sophie be celebrated and loved by so many. And it was a glimpse, ever so small, of the fairy tale unfolding for Sophie's life.

❈❈❈

I'm sure few would consider her story a fairy tale, with a fairy-tale ending.

When we think of fairy tales, we imagine something magical, "happily ever afters," sensational stories of love and excitement, rescue, and adventure with, of course, a beautiful soundtrack to go with it all. And when we think of fairy tales, we often assume they are for the storybooks.

Perhaps we imagine how they may come true for us. How our knight in shining armor may appear and sweep us off our feet, how our family will become everything we ever dreamed it would be or how our careers will be all we imagined them to be. But then disappointment strikes, reality sinks in, and we discover that our lives have not unfolded like we envisioned they would. Fairy tales don't come true in real life. Or do they?

Greater than the authors who write the best love stories, the best adventure stories, and the best fairy tales is The Author who created love, adventure, and the minds to write those fairy tales. I wonder if the longing and joy a fairy tale produces in our hearts serves to illuminate the reality that we are actually created for a happy ending. We are created for more than what this world seems to give us. Solomon, in Ecclesiastes, points to this reality, saying, "He has made everything beautiful in its time. Also, he has put eternity into man's heart" (3:11 ESV).

In the midst of the most "magical place on earth," the Lord was pointing me to Him and His Kingdom, reminding me that the joy and delight I longed to see my daughter experience firsthand at Disney, she would get to experience in far greater ways in heaven. And God allowed me to taste that joy with her through a magical day at Disney.

I knew God was writing a beautiful story for our little girl, one I didn't fully understand and one that was still being written. But oftentimes I thought of her story and how it affected my story instead of just thinking of her. As we celebrated her life at Walt Disney World, I only thought of her. Her story. Her celebration. Her fairy tale that God was so beautifully writing and weaving our friends and family and even strangers into the threads of.

It was more than just her story I was realizing, but His story, the Great Author's story, for our lives. Sophie's story had a "happily ever after." Her happily ever after would either be soon with Jesus where she would be in awe and wonder of all the glories of heaven and seeing Jesus face-to-face, or it would be later with Jesus if God chose to perform a miracle on her body.

Either way, her happily ever after wouldn't be on earth. And for those who know Jesus, our happily ever after is the day when He makes all things new, when He welcomes us into His kingdom and washes away the tears from our faces. It's the day where death will be no more and all that lies ahead of us will be joy. This life is important, and it is important to God, but it is not the end. It is only the beginning of a story, the greatest story of all being written by the One who created the ultimate love story of rescue and redemption—a story that includes for all believers the best happily ever after that we could ever imagine.

The process in which we experience that happily ever after is not how we would anticipate, but it is how fairy tales go. There is destruction and devastation and heartache in any good fairy story, but we always see the redemption of the destruction. And so it is with our own fairy story—though it can seem as if we only see the destruction, redemption is coming.

The great author J. R. R. Tolkien coined the term *euchatastrophe*. It means a "good" destruction. What a mysterious paradox!

He says in his essay "On Fairy Stories" of the resurrection of Jesus after His brutal death on the cross that, "The resurrection was the greatest 'eucatastrophe' possible in the greatest Fairy Story—and produces that essential emotion: Christian joy which produces tears because it is qualitatively so like sorrow, because it comes from those places where Joy and Sorrow are at one, reconciled, as selfishness and altruism are lost in Love."[1]

A eucatastrophe. A good destruction, slowly producing in us a "joy beyond the walls of the world, poignant as grief."[2] This journey with Sophie was doing just that, destroying us and pointing us to a joy whose recesses we had yet to realize ran so deep—a joy revealed in the Father's love for us.

# EIGHT

## THE FATHER'S LOVE

*For you created my inmost being;*
   *you knit me together in my mother's womb.*
*I praise you because I am fearfully and wonderfully made;*
   *your works are wonderful,*
   *I know that full well.*
*My frame was not hidden from you*
   *when I was made in the secret place,*
   *when I was woven together in the depths of the earth.*

   —Psalm 139:13-15 NIV

Mother's Day, the wonder of butterflies, and daddy-daughter dates. Things that should cause joy in the hearts of my daughter and our family but felt vulnerable to the weight of grief over Sophie's condition. Yet God had purpose even amid the weight of knowing these memories would be so momentary: to show His love, the love of a Father who can redeem anything.

I walked out to the kitchen that Mother's Day morning with a growing ache in my chest and quickly saw a bouquet of pink and yellow flowers, with a yellow card leaning against it on our kitchen counter. The word *MOMMY* was on the front as if written by a child. I was undone.

*Mommy.*

The word I would never hear my daughter say. The word that had become so much a part of my identity in such a short time. The thought of a day coming where I would be a mommy but not have my child with me was too much to bear. Mother's Day would be a different kind of celebration. It was one of those days where you enter the depths of your pain and grief while asking God to somehow enable you to take joy in these precious moments you get to have with the one you will have to say goodbye to soon. I didn't want to miss the sweetness of the day, but I couldn't wish away the pain either.

Kevin was committed that day to not only entering the emotions of the day but to making sure we also celebrated and enjoyed it as a family. Kevin came out, quickly enveloping me in his arms as he said "Happy Mother's Day" with such pride.

Something had switched in the way he looked at me and cared for me when I became pregnant. He'd always been protective, delighting in me as his wife, but I was seeing in him a different love. I was seeing a different love in both of us—the kind of love that moves beyond focusing on what this person gives to you and more toward a love growing in what we give, in what we are willing to sacrifice for the other.

I saw it as he looked at me, and I saw it as he spoke of our daughter and looked at my growing baby bump. Oh, how he loved this little girl growing inside of me! My love grew for him as I saw him freely give his love to her.

We sat on the couch as I opened the card and the beautifully wrapped square gift sitting beside it.

From inside the gift, I pulled out a booklet with the title *The Little Looking Bear*. On the front I noticed a photo of a bear that looked familiar and . . . wait . . . it said "by Kevin Dennis."

My brow furrowed, and then shock replaced my initial confusion as it registered that Kevin had written a book for Sophie and me.

"Wait, what? You wrote this?" I uttered through disbelief. I covered my eyes with the book while laughing and crying at the same time. I'm a master at that strange combination.

I hadn't even read it, but it didn't matter what words were in it. The mere fact he had written it displayed love to me in such a unique and sweet way. Kevin never ceases to amaze me.

The bear on the front was familiar because it was the bear we had just made at our local Build-A-Bear store. At our first ultrasound with Sophie, our doctor's office had given us a small recorder that we recorded Sophie's heartbeat to later place inside a teddy bear. Her heartbeat was always with us. At the time we had no idea it would be a heartbeat we would not always get to hear.

Earlier in the week, before Mother's Day, we had gone to the store, picked out a cute brown bear, watched them stuff it with cotton, and placed the recording of her heartbeat in the palm of the little bear's hand. We chose a pink and blue gingham dress with a pink polka-dot bow around the waist. It looked like Sophie to us.

---

Kevin stepped in and lifted my eyes to hope, to Christ, and to the celebration of my daughter's sweet life. He reminded me of the reality that Sophie had everything she needed for the story God was writing for her.

---

This book told a story of that bear. I could hardly get through the first page as I opened it and read with swelling pride what my husband had written:

> To my precious daughter, Sophia,
> and my beautiful wife, Lindsey,
> on Mother's Day.

No photos filled the pages in the book—that would come later. Each character in the book was a different animal that could be found somewhere in our home. Kevin and I would together photograph scenes with each of the animals that he would edit to appear as though they were drawn. In the end, we printed the book to take and read to Sophie at the hospital when she was born.

But for now, without photos and only words, I turned the page of the small white ring-bound booklet and read:

> Once there was a Little Bear
> who was looking for something.
> "I think I'm missing something," she said.
> "But I don't know what it is.
> I better go look for it."

*Missing something.* My first thought in that moment, *Yes, she's missing something . . . a brain, a skull—the very things she needs for survival.* I continued reading, wondering how Kevin would resolve this:

> So Little Bear went to her friend the Monkey
> and asked him, "Mr. Monkey, I think I'm missing
> something, but I don't know what it is.
> Can you help me look for it?"
>
> "Of course!" said the Monkey.
> "But what are you missing?
> You're certainly not missing beauty,
> because God made you with incredible beauty.
> So what could you be missing?"
>
> So Little Bear and Monkey kept on looking . . .

The book went on as Little Bear and Monkey gathered the buffalo that wondered if it was a strong heart the bear was missing, but the bear's heart was strong. Then there was a family of elephants who asked if it was wisdom the bear was looking for. But that wasn't it, for wisdom was in the bear's name. A little teddy joined the hunt wondering if it was love Little Bear was looking for, but that couldn't be it for the bear was surrounded by so many who loved her. And so the story ended as the whole crew of animals found Little Bear's Mama and Papa.

> "Mama and Papa, I think I'm missing some-
> thing," said Little Bear, "but I don't know what it
> is. Can you help me look for it?"
>
> "Of course, we would do anything for you!"
> said Mama and Papa. "But what are you missing?
> You're certainly not missing beauty,
> or a heart,
> or wisdom,
> or love.
> And you know what? You're not missing a home
> either, because your home is with us . . . and even
> better, we will always have a home with Jesus.
> So what could you be missing?"
>
> So Little Bear stopped looking because her
> friends and family helped her find that she
> already had everything she was looking for.

I thought Kevin would end the book with some kind of hopeful explanation for why she was missing something, me wanting some kind of concrete answers. Instead he pointed my eyes to the reality that God had given Sophie all she needed amid all it seemed she lacked. On that day, it wasn't our countless friends lifting my arms to hope, but my husband.

Kevin, knowing how I wrestled with why God would allow such brokenness in our life, in our daughter's life, stepped in and in a gentle and beautiful way lifted my eyes to hope, to Christ, and to the celebration of my daughter's sweet life. He reminded me of the reality that Sophie had everything she needed for the story God was writing for her.

That Mother's Day, and the following week, seemed as if God used each celebration to point me not only to the love of Sophie's earthly father, but the love of her heavenly Father, who was holding us as well.

❖❖❖

Butterfly week. That's what our good friends, Nick and Alicia, created for Sophie's twenty-seventh week of life. Nick was Kevin's roommate before we were married, and I was Alicia's roommate. They were married the same summer as we were and lived in the same apartment complex we did. We enjoyed countless fun memories together, experiencing the newness and joys of being newlyweds and navigating this new season of our lives.

---

The way Sophie's life would continue to unfold was unknown to us. But this we grasped more fully: that God was at work and in the most tangible of ways He was using His people to reveal His great love for her that extended beyond the reaches of our hearts.

---

They were friends who entered the joys of life and the deep sorrow with us. They were some of the first to come to our home and sit with us in tears as we shared Sophie's condition and this new journey we would take.

That Thursday, for week twenty-seven, they came over and presented us with a mobile that Alicia had made, full of hand-cut pink, yellow, and green butterflies, with a large S cut out and hanging from the middle. It came with a note to Sophie, teaching her the lesson of the butterfly. I was drawn to Alicia's correlation between God's Word and the story of the butterfly that she shared in her letter to Sophie:

When caterpillars are born, they have tiny cells inside their bodies that have all the information needed to build a butterfly. Caterpillars carry these cells with them everywhere they go—but the cells are so small, they don't even know they carry them! When the cocoon forms around them, the blueprints in these cells get rolled out and are used to construct the body, wings, legs, and antennae of a butterfly.

We find it absolutely amazing that these little guys are born with microscopic blueprints that have just one function—to transform a chubby little worm into an intricately designed butterfly. It reminds us of Ecclesiastes 3:11: "He has made everything beautiful in its time. He has also set eternity in the human heart; yet no one can fathom what God has done from beginning to end" (NIV).

God has set eternity in our hearts—"blueprints" of what we are meant to be: children of God. Little Sophie, do you know God has set eternity in your heart? He has designed you as a daughter—for a season you will be a daughter of Kevin and Lindsey and forever you will be a daughter of our Almighty God. You are precious in His sight, you are honored, and He loves you. (See Isaiah 43:4.)

If you saw a caterpillar in a cocoon and you didn't know what it was, you would think it would be rather strange. Why did this little guy decide to wrap himself up in a boring old blanket? He isn't moving—he might not even look alive! Yet LIFE is happening abundantly inside! You can't see it, but he is transforming into what he was made to be! But if you didn't know that, *you would wonder why the caterpillar didn't just go about its caterpillar life. But God knows the rest of the story—and if the caterpillar did in fact go about the rest of his life as a caterpillar, he would never experience life as a butterfly, beautiful and unique!*

*Sophie, right now we feel a little like we are looking at a cocoon for the very first time. We don't know why things are the way they are with your development. We don't know the rest of the story. But Sophie, we know by faith that LIFE is happening inside. We know that God has set eternity in your heart and that your blueprint is an irreversible design of beauty, love, and uniqueness that only our Lord can create.*

*Someone else lived a similar story long before your parents were even born. His name is Jesus. He also was wrapped in a cocoon, but it was in the form of a grave. Everyone who knew Him and loved Him was overcome with sorrow because they didn't know the whole story: that LIFE was conquering death so that we could live forever with the One who loves us the most out of anyone in this world. He emerged from His cocoon with great glory (even more glorious than a butterfly!), knowing the momentary sorrow was worth the everlasting joy of having us emerge from our own deaths by His grace. That's who your Savior is, Sophie. He creates life where none should exist. While we might not get to meet you on this side of heaven, we know that He loves you and has traded places with you so that you won't be in a cocoon forever. And we know that God is making something beautiful out of you, just like He does with butterflies.*

Kevin's little book and this letter served as striking reminders that God was still at work doing unseen things in our daughter's life. Even though there was so much Sophie was physically missing, I was reminded that the very blueprints of her life were written on her soul, a heart set for eternity.

⊗⊗⊗

The way Sophie's life would continue to unfold was unknown to us. But this we grasped more fully: that God was at work and in the most tangible of ways He was using His people to reveal His great love for her that extended beyond the reaches of our hearts.

---

Perhaps it is in that uncomfortable collision of joy and pain where the Father's love is displayed the most vividly. Isn't that how we see love displayed most vividly on the cross for us?

---

And no one continued to display that love more to her this side of heaven than her daddy, who with joy just a few days later crafted a daddy-daughter date for Sophie. Aided by the generosity of seventeen friends, they rallied together to give us the gift of her daddy taking Sophie to one of Epcot's finest and fanciest restaurants, Le Cellier, during their annual Flower and Garden Festival.

The evening began with Kevin presenting a beautiful orange rose corsage for Sophie to wear for the evening. How would she wear that? I'm glad you asked.

Kevin kneeled down in front of my belly, which was covered in a long red tunic, and pinned the corsage at the point of my shirt where my belly stuck out the most. I'm sure Sophie kicked when he pinned it there. I wasn't in the least embarrassed to walk through Epcot with a flower proudly pinned to my pregnant belly. This must have been a taste of parenthood where you unashamedly do embarrassing things for the sake of your child.

Kevin also presented Sophie with a small 5x7 card, a yellow flower printed in one corner, and the words "Sophie's Date with Daddy" on the top. On the card was a note telling Sophie how beautiful she was and spaces for a scavenger hunt with Daddy. We were to find the most beautiful flower, butterfly, and animal as we walked around Epcot before dinner.

That evening, we took photos in front of mirrors that obscured the reality of what we each looked like, namely even in my growing pregnant state I looked taller and skinnier than Kevin. I liked that. We traveled through the curtain of chains keeping all the butterflies in the butterfly exhibit. Butterflies landed on us, and we saw cocoons and butterflies about to come out of their cocoons: a picture of the blueprint, a reminder of Sophie's blueprint.

I saw a bunny hopping through the perfectly manicured bushes behind the England pavilion. Kevin and I decided that their peculiar-looking orange flowers were our favorites before heading to the main course.

Le Cellier is situated in the back of the Canada pavilion as if in a cellar. We walked down a dark corridor and into a small room full of tables, with men and women holding menus that had a little back glow to them so one could read the menu in the dimly lit room. Warm bread, grilled asparagus, their signature filet mignon, and a finish of maple crème brûlée satisfied our growing little girl and her momma. Daddy had chosen well and taken Sophie on the daddy-daughter date of her life. Later he would write of the day on my blog chronicling our story:

> I so deeply love my precious daughter, Sophie, and her amazing mom who is tirelessly taking care of her. I long to hold Sophie in my arms, and watch her grow, and take her on many special dates that help her know how beautiful God has made her. I long for those things with her on this earth, but I also know if God chooses for those things to wait until heaven, they will be all the more rich and pure and glorious in His great presence.

Kevin's beautiful words hardly came close to containing the magnitude of love I saw in his eyes toward Sophie. A doting father, doing all he could to love, cherish, and protect this growing baby inside of me. Kevin's little book, the story of the butterfly, and getting to watch Sophie's daddy take her on her first date were all a reflection of the Father's love for us.

❈❈❈

Perhaps it is in that uncomfortable collision of joy and pain where the Father's love is displayed the most vividly. Isn't that how we see love displayed most vividly on the cross for us? For the joy set before Him, Jesus our Savior endured the cross (Hebrews 12:2, paraphrase).

And this is how we know what love is, that Jesus laid down His life for us and so we are to lay down our lives for our brothers and sisters (1 John 3:16, paraphrase). Joy and pain colliding to point us to the love of the Father. And to point us to His love to our family through the countless men and women around us who continued to lay down their lives as they entered our story, brokenness, and celebrations.

# NINE

## THE COMING LOSSES

*Loss and death are only the preludes to gain and life.*

—Elisabeth Elliot

The weeks had moved quickly, too quickly, as my belly grew and we continued to watch our little girl grow and reveal her sweet and stubborn personality in the womb. I would lie on my side most nights, and if Sophie didn't like that side she'd push on my belly with her feet or hands or butt (I could never tell which body part) until I switched. Dancing to the beat of her own drum, I knew even in the womb she was just like me. Strong, stubborn, independent, and our little fighter. I loved that she was so much like me.

In the midst of all the celebrating, sadness had started to cloud most everything. I recognized the time was coming when these memories we were making with our daughter would be just that—memories. The cloud of sadness that hovered over us when we first found out Sophie's condition had lifted for much of the following months as people entered our lives and helped us celebrate Sophie's life.

> "If Sophie didn't have this condition, what would be erased from her story and her impact on the world?" What would we lose if Sophie wasn't Sophie? Could it be that what appears to be only impending loss may also produce gain?

Yet the closer Kevin and I came to her birth, the more difficult conversations we began to have, and the more painful questions we had to ask:

What do we want our time in the hospital to look like?

What supplies do we need?

What do we want to make sure we have of hers? Footprint molds? prints? locks of her hair?

What books do we want to bring to read to her?

What do we want to wear in our only photos with her?

What funeral home do we need to contact?

What outfit do we want to put her in? It will be her only one.

Such final and heartbreaking questions to ask as you anticipate the birth of your firstborn child. Such palpable losses awaited us.

❖❖❖

Our pastor, Renaut, and his wife, Brooke, took us out to celebrate Sophie's life as the weeks drew closer to Sophie's arrival. We met at a local bookstore, where they read to Sophie (and us) some of their favorite kids books and then purchased a few for us. Books like *Adventures of Frog and Toad*, Dr. Seuss's *My Many Colored Days*, and *The Giving Tree* by Shel Silverstein. They were books that made us laugh and held wisdom you wouldn't expect from children's books. Afterward, they took us to dinner and in true Renaut-like fashion asked us questions pointing our gaze upward:

- What have been some of your most powerful, wonderful moments since finding out you were pregnant?
- What are some of your greatest fears as you look ahead?
- What have been some of your darkest moments since finding out Sophie's condition?
- What ways have you been changed by this?

It was perfect timing as the weight of what was coming grew heavier and heavier on our minds. They were questions Kevin and I had not thought of, yet Renaut and Brooke created the space to see beyond the unique celebrations to the things God was doing in our hearts in the joys and the sorrows of the road we had been asked to walk. But there was one question from Renaut that stood out above the rest. It was more a thought than a question posed at some point during our conversation: "If Sophie didn't have this condition, what would be erased from her story and her impact on the world?" What would we lose if Sophie wasn't Sophie?

---

When the time comes that some of us will die, when the time comes that we will watch a loved one die, when the time comes when we will realize dreams have in fact not come to pass, when the time comes, you find the strength you need—just in time.

---

I hadn't thought of her life this way. It was powerful to think of all the things God had done in and through her life in just a few short months. Those things would all be erased if Sophie never had this condition. My mind was filled with all the loss to come, all we would lose with Sophie not here. Yet, what would I lose without her unfolding story in these moments?

Certainly I wanted Sophie whole and healed. I wanted that from the moment we went into that twenty-week ultrasound and all the moments afterwards. But if she was whole and healed, then everything after that ultrasound would not be a part of our story. All the people gathering around, all the ways God had used His people to draw us to Him and give us courage and strength, how we had been drawn deeper to the heart of God would be erased.

Of course we would have a different story of God's hand at work should this have been a pregnancy where she was healthy and would live. But we wouldn't have *this* story. The darkness of her diagnosis had ushered us into new and unexpected joys. So could it be even in the darkness of what awaited us, taunting us it seemed each day, there would be new joys to find?

Could it be that what appears to be only impending loss may also produce gain?

※※※

I had been praying that the Lord would give Kevin and me joy even amid the conversations we had to have as we stepped into the reality of what was coming. I wanted to continue to be able to celebrate her life and live in the reality of the day at hand. I wanted to trust that the strength the Lord gave us on the day we found out Sophie's condition, He would give a hundredfold on the day she would be born and whatever would unfold afterwards.

---

There began to be seeds of joy peeking their way out through the dirt. And these seeds came out of learning afresh to thank the Lord for what He had given us, even when I didn't feel thankful, even when I couldn't see how God would provide, and even when it felt that all was lost.

---

But it was far too easy to dwell on the loss that was coming and live in the fear of how we would walk through it. I remembered a story Corrie ten Boom tells in her book *The Hiding Place*. This book tells her story of being imprisoned in a Nazi concentration camp because she had hidden Jews, and in it she shares a conversation she had with her father when she was young just after witnessing the death of a baby—the frailty of life so apparent, causing her to begin to fear the loss of her loved ones.

> Father sat down on the edge of the narrow bed. "Corrie,"
> he began gently, "when you and I go to Amsterdam—
> when do I give you your ticket?"
> I sniffed a few times, considering this.
> "Why, just before we get on the train."
> "Exactly. And our wise Father in heaven knows
> when we're going to need things, too. Don't run out
> ahead of Him, Corrie. When the time comes that some
> of us will have to die, you will look into your heart and
> find the strength you need—just in time."[1]

When the time comes that some of us will die, when the time comes that we will watch a loved one die, when the time comes when we will realize dreams have in fact not come to pass, when the time comes, you find the strength you need—just in time. Not a moment before. Wasn't this the truth of those painful moments of finding out Sophie would not live? God had given grace for that moment and not a moment before. God gives us the strength to bear what He has asked us to bear when He asks us to bear it.

And so it would be the same on the day we would say goodbye to Sophie. He would give strength, in that moment. I wasn't sure how, I didn't need to know how. I needed His perspective for now. In these moments of such ache and fear, my heart was drawn to the cross.

What loss and what gain happened on the cross on that agonizing day over two thousand years ago? What did the resurrection mean for me now in this moment? It felt as if death surely wasn't defeated when Jesus rose from the dead, for it was consuming me.

Jesus spoke in John 6:39-40: "And this is the will of him who sent me, that I should lose nothing of all that he has given me, but raise it up on the last day. For this is the will of my Father, that everyone who looks on the Son and believes in him should have eternal life, and I will raise him up on the last day" (ESV). As I entered my third trimester and it felt like the beginning of the end, I wrote in my journal as I read that passage in John:

> *It feels like loss, all the Son had to go through, to lose Himself to gain. Yet He lost nothing. And so the promise is for us. In the same way that the will of the Father was that Jesus would lose nothing, but raise Him up on the last day—so we are given the promise that we who believe in Jesus will be raised up on the last day. We lose nothing and gain everything. Yet right now, the loss feels so deep, the coming loss of our daughter, the hope of a miracle.*
>
> *I am reminded today that in Christ we lose nothing. This is the hope of Christ, of heaven, of total redemption. We only gain as believers; we don't lose . . . even when the sorrows of life run too deep to fully see the gain. It is still coming. The losses we feel in this life will one day seem so insignificant—one day, perhaps not today. There is so much hope in that promise, so much richness in understanding the Father's will for us to lose nothing. Our view of loss is so temporal, so of this world and the Lord meets us in those places of temporal tunnel vision and continues to transform our mind, our understanding of Him, His love and His will. His heart is to give, not to take. And if it seems He takes more than gives, one day we will gain perspective on it all. His perspective. Eternal perspective. Perspective above our own.*

---

> I am convinced God calls us to thankfulness
> because it acknowledges our trust in Him
> and frees us from the bitterness that can so
> easily take root in our lives.

---

God was not giving me strength for the moments I feared, but strength and perspective for the moments I was experiencing. And in these moments, God began weaving in my heart a deeper trust in Him and a deeper understanding of His character.

In the waiting for the birth and death of my daughter, God continued to draw my heart back to Him as my anguish ebbed and flowed where I so quickly lost all the eternal perspective I had the day before (or even minutes before). There began to be seeds of joy peeking their way out through the dirt. And these seeds came out of learning afresh to thank the Lord for what He had given us, even when I didn't feel thankful, even when I couldn't see how God would provide, and even when it felt that all was lost.

I remembered this was in fact how our journey began with Sophie.

❈❈❈

"We need to thank the Lord for this." I had said those words through tears in the car the day after that twenty-week ultrasound. The shock of having just found out our daughter's diagnosis gave way to the bitter reality. I certainly didn't feel thankful in that moment, anything but. I felt sorrow and sadness and a suffocating ache in my lungs. But I remembered a story I had read a long time ago in a book by a man named Bill Bright. A man whose life was transformed by Jesus in his early twenties and went on to begin one of the largest nonprofit Christian mission organizations in the world.

The short book was titled *How You Can Walk in the Spirit*. At the end of this book Bill shares a story of a woman who came into his office who was going through great pain and grief over a friend who had died in a car accident. She had been the driver. He shared some Scripture and then asked her a simple question at the end of their conversation: "Have you thanked God since the loss of your loved one?"[2]

Slightly aghast at the question, I remember thinking, *I would never have the courage to challenge someone to a thankful heart in the thick of great pain.* But then I wondered to myself, *Am I convinced God really means to be thankful in all circumstances?* I reread what Paul says to the Thessalonians: "Rejoice always, pray continually, give thanks in all circumstances; for this is God's will for you in Christ Jesus" (1 Thessalonians 5:16-18 NIV).

Surely there must be a caveat to the word *all.*

Knowing the words were first written in Greek, I looked up the meaning of the word *all* in its original language. Not too surprised, I discovered the word used is the Greek word *pas*, which means: "individually, each, every, any, all, the whole, everyone, all things, everything."[3] It is not saying I get to selectively choose what to be thankful for, but to "give thanks" (which is a verb, and therefore an action, and therefore a choice to act on) in each individual circumstance God brings me into. Turns out you don't need to know Greek to understand that *all* means "all."

I knew the opposite of a thankful heart is an ungrateful and often bitter heart. I've heard it said before, "I've never met a bitter person with a thankful heart or a thankful person with a bitter heart." We all have probably rubbed shoulders with the people who complain about their lives and have been that person perhaps more often than we care to admit.

I wondered, as I read that story, what would it look like to have a heart transformed by praise? What would it look like to be honest about my feelings about our circumstances but continually drawn back to thankfulness to the One walking with us through our circumstances? I am convinced God calls us to thankfulness because it acknowledges our trust in Him and frees us from the bitterness that can so easily take root in our lives.

Somehow I knew, as Kevin and I sat in the car, I needed to acknowledge my trust in the One who knew what would unfold with our daughter amid all the questions and ache stirring in my heart. I didn't know how I would give thanks to begin this new journey, but I realized I needed to, so both of us prayed.

We prayed words of praise and thankfulness to the One we were convinced loves us and is good. We confessed our trust in Him while being honest about our fears and sorrow. We thanked Him for allowing us to walk this path and for how we knew He would walk it with us. We prayed God would continue to give us thankful hearts, a heart of praise in this season of great sadness.

❈❈❈

But as the weeks moved on, it became more difficult to choose thankfulness. It was easier to dwell on the coming pain and wish for a way out of it. Yet God continued to be faithful to answer that prayer that He would give us thankful hearts on this journey. I was challenged daily to give thanks; this was not (and is not now) my natural inclination.

> How strange! It was in choosing thankfulness, in wrestling with the coming losses, where God was revealing more of His character and inviting me to bring the "shackles" of my own heart to Him.

I was great at complaining, I was superb at dwelling on all the hard things, even amid all the wonderful celebrations and all the joy being infused into our pain. Still when I would lie on my bed trying to get comfortable from a belly that seemed to take over my body, at the end of a long day, my mind couldn't stop running to all that was ahead. It was easy to forget all the beauty God was painting in the midst of the pain.

Throughout each week of our pregnancy with Sophie, every night before Kevin and I would go to sleep we would pray and thank the Lord for the day. Each night was a fight to choose thankfulness, to look for things to thank the Lord for rather than complain.

And I noticed as I fought to be thankful that, though I still daily asked why, my heart was not growing bitter. I was only growing more thankful that God held the answers to my whys. It was a daily, moment-by-moment choice of thankfulness. And it was a choice I had to make out of faith, despite what I felt.

Hebrews 12:15 says, "See to it that no one falls short of the grace of God and that no bitter root grows up to cause trouble and defile many" (NIV). How quickly the seed of bitterness is able to take root.

---

> For as I thanked God I began seeing all
> He was giving, all the gain in the midst of
> the loss, and all that was joy in the
> midst of the sorrow.

---

The daily choice was this: Will I in faith choose thankfulness or sit in my pity party? Ungratefulness is a thief of joy. Thankfulness leads me to deep joy. Every day I didn't choose thankfulness I was so quickly robbed of any kind of joy.

So the further I began to be in my pregnancy I began to thank God that He had chosen Kevin and I to walk this journey. I began to thank Him that in His infinite wisdom He had allowed our little girl to have anencephaly. I thanked Him for what was and not what I feared would come. In the final weeks of carrying Sophie, I thanked God that I had a daughter who was alive and with us. I thanked Him for the simple and sweet family moments where Kevin and I would just sit in bed, watching Sophie kick, reading to her, talking to her. I thanked God that He was at work, doing something far greater in and through all three of our lives than we could ever imagine.

In the devotional *Streams in the Desert*, Lettie Cowman writes a response to God's Word in 2 Chronicles: "As they began to sing and praise, the LORD set ambushes against the men . . . who were invading Judah, and they were defeated" (20:22 NIV).

Cowman goes on to say:

> Oh, that we could reason less about our troubles, and sing and praise more! There are thousands of things that we wear as shackles which we might use as instruments with music in them, if we only knew how.
>
> Those men that ponder, and meditate, and weigh the affairs of life, and study the mysterious developments of God's providence, and wonder why they should be burdened and thwarted and hampered—how different and how much more joyful would be their lives, if, instead of forever indulging in self-revolving and inward thinking, they would take their experiences, day by day, and lift them up, and praise God for them.[4]

My shackles of pain, grief, and knowing I would most likely have to bury my firstborn daughter became the instruments to move my heart to praise. How strange! It was in choosing thankfulness, in wrestling with the coming losses, where God was revealing more of His character and inviting me to bring the "shackles" of my own heart to Him.

Each question of my heart that I invited God into would open a new door to hope and a new avenue to knowing Him more clearly. I was not thankful because I felt like every part of this story was good or made sense. I was thankful because I knew the One who was good in everything and I knew the One who understood why all of this was happening. I didn't have to understand to be thankful or even *feel* thankful to be thankful; I could simply in faith thank the One who did understand. And because He was in control of my circumstances, I could thank Him for my circumstances.

These were significant truths God was writing and forging on my heart in the midst of the celebrating, in the midst of the waiting, and in the midst of the suffering. He was forging it on the days where I was reluctant to praise Him and on the days where praise came with ease. And in the forging, my heart was turning to hope.

For as I thanked God I began seeing all He was giving, all the gain in the midst of the loss, and all that was joy in the midst of the sorrow. Truth be told, as we began this new journey with Sophie, all I had imagined was the sorrow and pain ahead of me. I'm pretty sure I wouldn't have believed you if you had told me this new journey would also contain so much joy.

# TEN

## The Unimagined Joy

*If my life is broken when given to Jesus*
*it's because pieces will feed a multitude*
*while a loaf will satisfy only a little lad.*

—Ruth Stull

We could, of course, keep our celebrations to ourselves, our brokenness hidden from others, our questions and pain solely brought before the foot of the cross. And I'm confident God would have still brought healing. But long ago, when I read the words of Stull, I became convicted that my life and my brokenness were not meant for my growth and healing alone, but so others could know and see the life-saving words of my Savior: living and active in me and offered to others.

If my life was to fall apart in pieces, I at least wanted the pieces to be my offering. If it was all I could offer, it was still something. And it was these small broken pieces that God began to multiply as the audience of Sophie's life and celebration continued to grow as I chronicled her story and celebrations on my blog.

At that point in my life, when I looked back to that day when we found out our daughter wouldn't live, I couldn't imagine the joy that would rise in the midst of the pain. I had known of others who had suffered the loss of their babies to stillbirth or miscarriage and the words "I could never go through that" had been the internal response of my heart. And now, although in a much different way, I, too, was about to walk through the loss of a child.

---

It's an invitation to trust that God is at work in unseen ways writing a story we are mere participants of, telling a story of His grace, His mercy, and His power. A story to which He invites not only us but also those around us.

---

Yes, I couldn't imagine this for my life. I couldn't imagine the intensity of pain I was experiencing, or even suffering these things without the grace of God. And I couldn't imagine the community that would rally around us. I couldn't imagine how laughter or smiles would exist alongside knowing I would lose my daughter.

I could not have dreamed that a little girl I would carry that no one had seen (apart from those ultrasound photos) would have such an impact on those around us, that she would be so loved by family, friends, and even strangers. We cannot walk through a tragedy and see joy arise during it without God's grace to give us eyes to see past the pain. Often in the anticipation of tragedy, or even in the middle of it, all we can see are the ashes. But here in Sophie's story God never seemed to stop lifting our eyes above the ashes to remind us He makes beauty out of ashes.

❖❖❖

Each week beauty rose out of our ashes as friend after friend and even stranger after stranger entered our story and helped us celebrate the life of this little girl. Even the Fairy Godmother (yes, you read that right) who had followed our story after sprinkling that "obscene" amount of pixie dust on me at the Magic Kingdom had been captivated by our butterfly week and sent us tickets to a park known for its butterflies. Countless people began entering our lives left and right to lift our arms to celebrate.

Friends gave us gifts to go out to nice dinners and tickets to see dolphins and whales up close at SeaWorld. My friend Jen, who played Nemo in the *Finding Nemo* show, organized a day at the Animal Kingdom where we had VIP seats at several shows and met the entire cast after each one. And one of my most empathetic friends, Adrienne, gifted us a box full of thirty fun kid things to do for Sophie's thirtieth week of life: puzzles, books, Go Fish cards, jump ropes all included (though I wouldn't recommend jumping rope for pregnant women—or at least wear Depend undergarments if you try).

I played Go Fish that week with Ruth, the three-year-old daughter of some close friends. She had fallen in love with Sophie and would often come up and touch my belly while smiling and saying with great affection, "You're just so cute, Sophie." I loved that Sophie had little-kid friends who treated her like one of them—even in the womb.

We met a couple, Rebecca and Josh, who also carried a little girl, Savannah, with the same condition as Sophie. They became dear friends as we navigated the muddy waters of grief and joy intertwined together. Rebecca and I enjoyed speaking freely about the discomforts and joys of pregnancy while experiencing fear of what was coming. We even took our two little girls to their first rocket launch! And Josh received tickets to get as close as you can get to a rocket launch as a civilian. It was a blast. But Rebecca and I are convinced our little girls slept right through it.

No, I couldn't have imagined this. And I couldn't have imagined being serenaded by a boy band at thirty-two weeks with Sophie while on stage in front of nearly eighteen thousand people.

We have no categories for how God will work in and through His people when He asks us to walk through something we thought we would never have to face. But this is a part of the invitation to joy in the face of suffering. And it's an invitation to trust that God is at work in unseen ways writing a story we are mere participants of, telling a story of His grace, His mercy, and His power. A story to which He invites not only us but also those around us.

I'm sure you want to hear how a boy band was invited into our story, right?

It's one of my favorite parts.

✸✸✸

A few weeks before my thirty-second week of pregnancy, my brother Dan came to visit. He's the one in our family who will drop everything at a moment's notice to be with family in time of need. He also has a cool job working in the music industry in New York City. We made memories with Sophie that week, and he did fun uncle things like beating her at miniature golf. (Perhaps her mom was more of the weak link.)

Dan and I headed out for lunch after he beat me at mini golf, and he casually said, "Guess who I got to hang out with last week?"

"Probably someone famous. Who?" I asked, knowing my brother and a question like that often ended with someone famous.

Dan exclaimed, "Some guys from 98 degrees!" knowing of my unabashed love for boy bands.

"No way . . . you know they're coming to Orlando soon?"

Dan replied with the words he realized I unapologetically hoped he would say: "Really? I know someone who does their social media. Maybe I could get you tickets."

I felt giddy with excitement at the mere possibility.

We laughed and talked about what a fun memory that would be with Sophie, to take her to her first boy band concert.

Dan later contacted their social media director, Jade, who is as cool as her name sounds, and told her our story. She was inspired and said she'd love to help get us tickets, a meet and greet, and maybe something else special. I was given a heads-up as to what may be included in that something special. And the mere idea of it made me incredibly nervous.

There is a point in the concert where they invite four women onto the stage and serenade them with the song "My Everything." Jade had pitched the idea of me being one of those women. Picturing being serenaded in front of an audience of thousands sent shivers down my spine; I hate being put on the spot, but what a memory that would be. I would do it for Sophie; I would do anything for her.

So I said nothing and decided to wait and see what would happen.

Kevin, who is not so much of a boy band guy, embraced the excitement of it all. And together we made matching black T-shirts that had "#celebratingsophie" printed on the back. Mine also had a pair of white headphones printed on the front, perfectly framing my protruding belly, with the words: "32 weeks old. I've got a fever. It's 98 Degrees.—Sophie" printed in between the earpieces of the headphones.

I am shameless.

Jade had told the band our story, and we wrote a note to them from Sophie thanking them for being a part of her story and making it so special.

When we arrived at the Orlando Amway Center, I'm not sure I realized how many people would be at this concert. Not only was 98 Degrees performing but also Boyz II Men (whose songs I must confess I have almost memorized) and New Kids on the Block. We walked in . . . step by step.

The arena was filled with thousands of middle-aged women acting like teenagers again. It was comical. Kevin and I stood in the VIP line as we waited to be escorted to the room where we'd meet the band. Nervous and feeling a bit like an imposter, I didn't even know the names of all the guys in the band.

*What are we doing here?* I thought.

I tried not to let on my ignorance to the forty or fifty mega fans in that small room with us. People smiled and laughed as they saw my shirt, and Kevin got out his camera when the time came for the band to enter the room. We at least looked the mega-fan part.

And then we were mesmerized and crazy along with the rest of the group when Nick, his brother, Drew, Jeff, and Justin entered the room with smiles and waves. We all erupted with cheers and screams so loud that you would have thought we were already in the arena.

We stood in line, me nervously waiting our turn to get their autograph and give them the note we had written. What do you say to famous people? I had never met one before.

They were so kind and down to earth, and it turns out you just talk to them like a normal person because they're just like the rest of us. Except famous.

Kevin and I took photos with them and chatted a bit. Jeff remembered hanging out with Dan, told me to tell him hi, and then we were escorted down to the main floor where we had seats about six rows back from the center stage.

The stage was in the middle of the arena with another stage on the opposite side, and a walkway that connected the two. Our seats were along that walkway, and if I wanted to be the crazy fan reaching my hands up to the stage while the band performed, I could have just gone up there from my seat. I didn't.

When Boyz II Men came out, I almost did.

There were close to eighteen thousand people there that night. The atmosphere was electric. 98 Degrees performed first, and I wondered if I would be pulled up for their serenade song. Nerves kept me from fully enjoying their first few songs, part of me hoping I wouldn't be placed on the stage. Jade had said nothing about it, so I thought nothing would happen. A few more songs passed, and just as my heart started to calm, I looked to my right and Jade held out her hand, motioning me to come with her.

My heart lurched in my chest. I took a deep breath and thought, *Oh, dear, here we go.*

Kevin followed, and we were taken to the gate that kept people from going up to the stage. There a hefty man with black hair spiked up in ten or twelve sections down the middle of his head, each spike about ten inches high, opened the gate with a smile, letting Kevin and me into a small seat at the base of the stage.

Kevin would sit there while I went on stage. The guy with the spiky hair noticed I was nervous and said, "Just breathe; Nick Lachey is pretty dreamy, isn't he?"

Even amid my nerves, I didn't miss a beat and said, "Oh, I'm OK... my husband is much dreamier."

The time came, and the guys came off the stage from their last song to grab the girls that had been chosen. There I went, escorted up the stairs by Justin (we were on a first-name basis by then) in the middle of an arena filled with thousands, hoping I wouldn't fall over as I tried to get my slightly off-balance, pregnant self up onto the small stool that each of us sat on in each corner of the stage.

Women who had lost all inhibitions reached out their hands at the base of the stage shouting, "I wish it was me up there! You're so lucky!" I still felt like an imposter, and I still couldn't remember all of their names, but at that moment I didn't care. We were celebrating Sophie and making a memory I would have never imagined we would make just a couple of months earlier.

I just wanted to take her to a boy band concert, and here I was on stage about to be serenaded by one.

As the guys sang the song "My Everything" they rotated around so that each of the four women on stage had a chance to be serenaded by each band member. The women at the base of the stage went slightly ballistic when Nick came over, knelt down in front of me, held my hand, looking straight into my eyes—singing a love song.

I'm not going to lie, it was awkward—me pregnant, with my husband seated just a few feet away, being sung this romantic song. I laugh just thinking about it.

Still full of nerves on stage as each guy came around to sing to me, I decided the normal thing to do (do I sing along or just sway?) would be talk to them.

People, I talked to them while they were trying to sing. And I didn't just talk, I asked them questions! I'm sure they thought I was crazy.

As the song ended and I was escorted off the stage, pure joy erupted on my face, on Kevin's face, as we both thought, *What just happened?* Jade later told us that the band had been impacted by our story. I don't know how they were impacted, but I always wondered how God would use Sophie's life in the most unlikely ways and places. Even here, at a boy band concert, God was inviting the most unlikely people into our story, reminding us that even in the painful chapters of our story, there is much joy to be found.

❈❈❈

The following week was week thirty-three. We were still coming off the euphoria of being at the concert when a large and heavy package arrived in the mail from my mother-in-law, Kathy.

The celebrations of Sophie's life were incredible, at times surreal, at other times quite simple. Some were filled with laughter, some with tears, and most with threads of both. Each one of them was a reflection of the people who loved and cared for us. Each one created lasting memories. And each one, led by the Lord, gave us exactly what we needed when we needed it.

We opened it, pulling out a beautiful quilt that had been put together by many of our friends and family for Sophie. It was filled with squares that had each been handmade and crafted with love. Each square had a story behind it, down to even the history of the materials used on some of the squares. There were pieces of fabric from Kevin's baby blanket and my wedding dress. Footprints of Sophie's cousins expressing their love graced one square. A crown stitched with care, reflecting Sophie's identity as a daughter of the King of Kings, filled another square made by my mom and dad. And a whole square with the signature of every princess at Walt Disney World. Over thirty squares covered that large quilt, each put together by a family member or friend. Kevin and I were in shock as we looked at each square. The thoughtfulness, love, and time spent on this quilt overwhelmed us with thankfulness! What a way to start Sophie's thirty-third week!

Kathy (Sophie's Mammo and my mother-in-law), one of the biggest gift-givers I know, came up with the idea. She somehow rallied many of our friends and family, sending them all the materials they would need to make their own squares. She then gathered the quilt patches and pieced them together. A local quilt shop then added stitching to bring the whole piece together. Sophie's name, in beautiful script, is stitched along each side of the quilt.

Kathy told us later that when she brought it to the quilt shop, she discovered that it would take several weeks to make and may not be ready in time for Sophie's thirty-third week. But when she told them our story, they rushed her order and put it at the top of the list to make sure we had it as soon as possible. I met these quilters years later and discovered that these women shed many tears over their stitches for us. They had been drawn into our story, loving our daughter, Sophie, and the children who would follow with a love that moved my heart to again wonder at all the unseen ways God is at work in the chapters of our lives. Unseen and unimaginable ways.

❈❈❈

The celebrations continued, from baking cookies, to Fourth of July water-balloon fights, to flying kites on the beach, to painting works of art.

Somehow as the weeks progressed, friends knew we would need our eyes lifted up more frequently and need greater space to process our pain and what was coming. So when my friend Jess celebrated our thirty-ninth week with us by presenting a large book filled with promises God had made to others in their own times of sorrow and pain, it was a beautiful offering of hope to our weary hearts.

When week forty approached (what I thought would be my final week of pregnancy), Julie, her husband, Danny, and Julie's parents sent us to one of my now-favorite restaurants in Orlando. It's a hidden restaurant on a large lake. You can sit and enjoy a drink in Adirondack chairs overlooking the water while you wait for your table, or you can just spend the evening out there by the fireplace or sitting on the dock.

Kevin and I sat on the dock before we headed inside to eat, looking out at the vast expanse of water, small juts of land, and homes peeking out in the distance as the sun slowly set. Peaceful and calm, it was exactly what we needed as we neared Sophie's birth. Julie apologized that it wasn't more dramatic of a celebration, or more creative. I told her, "But it was what we needed."

My entire family all flew in around week forty, not knowing when Sophie would arrive and wanting to be here to meet her. My brother Luke flew in a day before the rest, and in true Luke fashion, he infused the laughter that we needed, coming with supplies for a pedicure. And in a scene I'll probably never see again, Kevin, Luke, and I all sat at the edge of our tiny tub giving each other foot scrubs and pedicures. And after our feet were as smooth as butter, we huddled together on our deep comfy couch and watched a Disney princess movie. It's safe to say that Sophie's extended family would do anything for her.

A few days later, Kevin and I headed to where my parents were staying and opened the door to see a fantastical surprise tea party that my mother—ever the party planner—put on. Everyone wore giant colorful tissue-paper hats, and pretty pink décor hung everywhere. The tables were set as if anticipating royalty, and almost our entire family was there: my parents, in-laws, all of my siblings, and my nephews.

At the end of this party, my family gathered us into the living room and pulled out gifts. It was a surprise shower, since we did not have a typical one in light of Sophie's condition. It had been one of the many things I was sad not to experience. This one, however, revealed that our family was gathering behind us to give us gifts of faith. Faith that God would heal Sophie and faith that together as a family, we would trust God for whatever would unfold.

❈❈❈

The celebrations of Sophie's life were incredible, at times surreal, at other times quite simple. Some were filled with laughter, some with tears, and most with threads of both. Each one of them was a reflection of the people who loved and cared for us. Each one created lasting memories. And each one, led by the Lord, gave us exactly what we needed when we needed it.

The amazing part about Sophie's life and celebrations was not the extravagance of them, but the people who surrounded us in them and chose to value and celebrate Sophie's life with us. The celebrations, small and large, served to not only create memories for us but to reveal to those who were watching, who were in the celebrations themselves that our God can make beauty out of ashes.

God was taking my small offering of pain and brokenness and transforming me and others around me in the midst of the great sorrow. I could not have imagined the depth of sorrow the diagnosis of Sophie would usher me into, but I also could not have imagined the joy. And I wondered as I knew the weekly celebrations would eventually end, what kind of beauty God would continue to write and what kind of joy He would give in the midst of meeting and perhaps saying goodbye to my firstborn daughter.

# ELEVEN

## THE EXPLOSION OF LOVE

*O love of God, how strong and true,*
*eternal and yet ever new,*
*uncomprehended and unbought,*
*beyond all knowledge and all thought.*
*O heavenly love, how precious still*
*in days of weariness and ill,*
*in nights of pain and helplessness,*
*to heal, to comfort, and to bless.*

—Horatius Bonar

I was forty-two weeks pregnant and having a hard time sleeping, moving, and basically doing anything as my belly overwhelmed my 5'3" frame. Sophie had been due on August 15, but as that date had come and gone she didn't seem to be too eager to come out of the safe confines of my womb. And to be honest, as uncomfortable as I was, nothing in me wanted to let her. She was safe, alive, and well inside of me. And as soon as her body broke free into the fresh air of this world, her time in it would be short. I longed to meet her face-to-face, but I longed for her to be with me for, well, forever.

I wondered if my longing for her was a glimpse of the Father's love and longing for me?

Kevin and I arrived at the hospital late the evening of August 28, nervous, fearful, and hopeful. I would be induced. So many emotions ran through both of us as I put my hospital gown on and sat on the hospital bed in the large corner room covered with windows. This would be the room I would welcome my daughter in, and this might be the room where I said goodbye.

My family arrived, and my two brothers, sister, mom, and dad gathered around my hospital bed. Tears in all of our eyes, Kevin at my side, we prayed. My dad, who has always lifted our eyes to worship, led us in Matt Redman's song "10,000 Reasons." We sang the lyrics "Whatever may pass and whatever lies before me, let me be singing when the evening comes" with hope that we would still bless the Lord, we'd still praise His name in whatever He asked us to endure next.

Thousands of prayers had been lifted for us, for our little girl, and all of it led to worship. Worship. To give God the praise He is due. Praise He is due not because of what He would do or would not do, but because of Who we know He is. Worthy. No matter what would unfold, my eyes were fixed on Jesus in both weariness and strength.

Unknown to us in that moment, a little army of prayer warriors had gathered in the lobby below. At any given time, twenty-five to thirty-five people from our church were covering our family and us in prayer and in celebration of Sophie's life. They all wore buttons from Walt Disney World that said "Celebrating Sophie." And each member of my family there wore a colorful shirt that said "Celebration" from the nearby town of Celebration. And whether through buttons or T-shirts, worship songs or prayer, when fear began to overwhelm us, God would bring another person, another story of how He was at work to remind us of His care for us.

The medications began, and while I was still able to walk around, Kevin and I took a short walk down the hall to get tea. A nurse noticed me at the tea and coffee station and began to say "Congratula—" but stopped herself short and asked what room we were in. She immediately knew who we were and spoke words of encouragement to us, as she shared the impact that our lives already had on the nursing staff through the birth plan we had written before we arrived. Our birth plan included our desire to trust God with our daughter's life, valuing and celebrating her life for however she would come and however long she would stay.

The nurses communicated awe of our view of the value of life, our choice to celebrate this little girl and honor the life God gave her. Nurses who didn't know God expressed intrigue at how we spoke of God in our birth plan. Again, these timely words lifted my heart from the sadness that continued to try to overwhelm me and reminded me that the Lord was still using Sophie's little life to bring great glory to Himself.

---

Those moments in labor were painful and yet beautiful—beautiful in the ways God was writing His truth in my heart, in the pain and not apart from it, in the truth of His presence, His love, His power, and His control. My heart began to be resolved to soft surrender as I continued to labor.

---

Several hours later, another nurse, Doreen, walked into our room and told us she had followed our story online and hoped that perhaps we would deliver there. A gift throughout the course of my labor, she held my hand and provided comfort in some of the darkest and most painful moments, and she rejoiced with us at the most joyful. Each nurse we encountered, whether for a few moments or twelve hours, blessed us with their words, presence, and care.

⬧⬧⬧

Labor intensified, and my doula, another Doreen, coached Kevin on how to help me manage my pain through the contractions. I chose not to get an epidural for a variety of reasons. But one of those, as strange as it may sound, was because I wanted to labor *with* Sophie. I wanted to experience the pain of labor. I wanted to feel physically what I was feeling emotionally.

The Pitocin slowly increased, and my contractions began to be two to three minutes apart with no relief for hours upon end. Every wave of pain concentrated almost fully in my lower back. Any movement produced an excruciating amount of agony.

Exhausted and at times delirious, at one point I couldn't stop thinking of losing Sophie, and fear took over. I almost lost control of the pain of my contractions, the grief pouring out of me. I remember saying, "I don't want to release her," as a torrent of tears poured out and overwhelmed me. My breath became difficult to catch as wave after wave of pain and fear flowed through my body. Safe and alive in my womb, would my precious daughter be safe outside?

Could I trust God with her life when it was so much more obvious how out of control I was of her life? There was an illusion of control as I carried her, that somehow I was her protector. All along God had been her Protector. Goodness, He had created her and sustained her this entire time. But that seemed so much more real when she would be outside of me.

---

As Kevin and I prayed, we sensed God's peace that though this was not the way we planned, He was still in control, and we could trust Him. His no would be His provision as well as His yes.

---

A friend sent Kevin a timely text in that moment with a verse from Isaiah that he began to read to me as I fought to catch my breath and regain control of my contractions.

> But now, thus says the LORD, your Creator, O Jacob, and
> He who formed you, O Israel, Do not fear, for I have
> redeemed you; I have called you by name; you are Mine!
> *When you pass through the waters, I will be with you*; and
> through the rivers, they will not overflow you. When you
> walk through the fire, you will not be scorched, Nor will
> the flame burn you. For I am the LORD your God, the
> Holy One of Israel, your Savior . . . Do not fear, for I am
> with you. (Isaiah 43:1-5, emphasis mine)

"Again," I said through tears and physical pain. And Kevin would read it again, with conviction.

"Again." Over and over I would say, "Again . . . read it again," until I believed every word of what he read.

I imagined, while hearing the words over and over, they were less about God being with me, but God being with Sophie. "When Sophie passes through the waters, I will be with her . . . do not fear, for I am with HER." I feared when Sophie would pass through my very literal waters. My waters protected her, and I could not release her. But God began releasing me, to trust Him that He loved and cared for my little girl with greater depth than I ever could. Those moments in labor were painful and yet beautiful—beautiful in the ways God was writing His truth in my heart, in the pain and not apart from it, in the truth of His presence, His love, His power, and His control. My heart began to be resolved to soft surrender as I continued to labor.

---

At every turn of this journey it seemed as if
God was beckoning me to travel with Him
through uncharted territories, to face my
fears and learn to trust that He would hold
me in the middle of all the unknowns.

---

My sister, Laurie, whose gentle presence can calm any room, told this story later as the song "Oceans" came on while I labored:

> One of my favorite memories is of how sweetly surrendered my sister was during labor and delivery. She was at the peak of her labor (twenty-seven hours in, contractions every two to three minutes, past complete exhaustion). This song comes on, and Linds starts softly singing the words to this song as it played in the room. It was so beautiful to watch my sister in the thick of labor continually seeking the Lord.

I have no recollection of those moments and was surprised this happened. I'm thankful Laurie remembered, and I'm thankful for the Lord's nearness in the midst of great pain, turning my heart to Him even when I wasn't aware of it!

At every centimeter I dilated, Laurie and her kids would make me a piece of artwork to put on the wall, congratulating me! A red balloon with "Yay, 5 cm . . . keep going." Another one with "6cm . . . almost there." But it became evident after thirty hours of continuous contractions, no sleep, and only 6 centimeters dilated that I wasn't progressing.

---

I do believe God renews promises to His people, reminding them of who He is, what He has done, and what He will do. God's Word is full of Him reminding His people of His promises.

---

The last thing we wanted to have was a C-section. It had been at the top of our prayer list: "Pray we don't have to have a C-section." And it would be another no from the Lord. I was concerned that with all the pain medication from a C-section, I would not be able to be fully present with Sophie and would forget my time with her. But Dr. K expressed concern that if they allowed my labor to continue, I would not have the energy to push. She didn't want to have to use forceps to pull Sophie out, since Sophie's head was so fragile. I loved that she not only took into account my health and safety but cared for this little life inside of me.

As Kevin and I prayed about this decision, we sensed God's peace that though this was not the way we planned, He was still in control, and we could trust Him. His no would be His provision as well as His yes.

❦❦❦

The time it took to be prepped and wait for surgery provided sweet time for Kevin and me to sit in our hospital room alone and prepare our hearts for what awaited. Kevin cuddled up next to my forty-two week pregnant body, hand on my belly in the little hospital bed, and we took eight minutes to listen to the song "Oceans" that had become so meaningful to us. Again, a fresh peace washed over us, knowing the time had come and Sophie would soon arrive. It was 11 p.m. on August 31, and as we looked at the clock and waited for the anesthesiologist we realized, much to our surprise, that our little Sophie might in fact be a September baby.

One of our initial prayers when we found out Sophie's diagnosis was that she would make it to full term, as babies with her condition can often come early. We had hoped that she would make it to August at the very least, if not her due date, and here we were about to enter September. God answered that prayer with a resounding and sweet yes.

My nurses walked me to the operating room, Kevin at my side, along with our photographer, Amanda, and videographer, Scott. Both of them worked with an organization called Now I Lay Me Down to Sleep that offers free and beautiful photography for parents who lose a child in childbirth, and in our case, could be there to capture every moment God would give us with a child who would most likely not live. The gift of their skills and presence was priceless to us.[1]

In that moment, I glimpsed the Father's love for me, how His heart must explode with love every time He intricately weaves a new creation in the secret places of a mother's womb.

It was a cold and sterile white room, and I was scared (Kevin, Amanda, and Scott had to wait outside while I was given an epidural and prepared for surgery). My nurse, Doreen, stood in front of me, holding my hand as the song "Oceans" once again played softly in the background on the playlist they allowed us to have in the room: "Where feet may fail and fear surrounds me, you've never failed and you won't start now."

At every turn of this journey it seemed as if God was beckoning me to travel with Him through uncharted territories, to face my fears and learn to trust that He would hold me in the middle of all the unknowns.

I felt so alone sitting on that cold operating table, and yet I was reminded that God was with me, that He was my anchor, that He was my hope. I could trust Him with whatever He asked me to walk through next, for He had not failed me yet. And I knew He would not fail me in whatever would come. These moments were such sacred moments, where the very presence of God broke through that hard and cold room and enveloped me with His love and power. "He gives strength to the weary, and to him who lacks might He increases power" (Isaiah 40:29). Never did I know the full extent of the promise of those words more than at that moment, alone but not alone, on the operating table.

I had no idea that right before I went into surgery all of the nurses had gathered to pray. And I had no idea that during our surgery many had stayed to pray for us, while still our church community prayed in the waiting area below. Once again the prayers of those around us strengthened our faith. God's power was flowing through us not because of our strength but because of the collective strength of His people gathered together to join hands and bear the weight of our pain and plead with God on our behalf. How true it is that God did not design us to do life on our own, but that a large part of the way we grow and are strengthened is through community.

The epidural took quick effect, and the bottom half of my body went numb. Kevin was ushered in, rushing to my side, gripping my left hand, looking into my eyes, and praying with intensity as the C-section began. My eyes had never been so fixed on Jesus, my whole being had never felt so dependent, so full of anticipation of what we were about to see Him do. And I trusted Him completely in that moment for whatever yes or no He would answer to our prayers for healing, for time.

A friend told me weeks before that she believed God was going to make a new promise to me when Sophie was born. I pondered that. I don't believe God makes new promises to us, for His Word is full of so many already that we struggle to remember and cling to. But I do believe God renews promises to His people, reminding them of who He is, what He has done, and what He will do. God's Word is full of Him reminding His people of His promises.

This idea of a renewed promise flooded momentarily into my mind as my ears became attuned to a song playing softly in the background. I had heard none of the music playing aside from "Oceans" when I was first brought into the room. But as I lay there, shivering, nervous, fearful, excited, I felt pressure in my stomach and heard the word *newborn* in the song faintly playing in the operating room. And then just as quickly, I heard Dr. K say with joy, "She's here!" as she pulled Sophie from my belly. The blue curtain was quickly drawn down in front of my face, and I saw her—arms stretched wide as if finally free from the confines of my womb, a small whimper from her little lips, and an explosion of love in my heart.

The split second of disappointment when I could see that God had not chosen to heal her was then tempered by the reality that she was alive! This was the prayer I had believed He would truly answer, that He would give us time with her. And though His no to her full healing brought disappointment, His yes to giving us time filled my heart with such awe that all disappointment in that moment slipped away.

They couldn't bring her to me fast enough. I didn't understand how such love could pour out of someone's heart, but there I was, totally enamored of this little girl I had grown to know and love in my womb and now saw with my eyes. All of her—her little toes and feet, her precious nose and lips, her sweet eyes, and, yes, even all the brokenness I could see in her—filled my heart with love for her. I knew it would be worth it to carry her, to go through the pain of birthing her, but I didn't know until then how worth it it all really was.

And I loved her not for what she could give to me. I loved her not because of anything she had to offer but simply because she was mine, woven in my womb, carried with sacrifice and longing, and wanted so badly as my own. In that moment, I glimpsed the Father's love for me, how His heart must explode with love every time He intricately weaves a new creation in the secret places of a mother's womb. My eyes flooded with love when I saw Sophie face-to-face for the first time. When did my Creator see me face-to-face for the first time? Even before I was woven in the womb says the prophet Jeremiah: "Before I formed you in the womb I knew you" (Jeremiah 1:5 NIV).

God was intimately acquainted with me before I had the ability to do a single thing. Before I had anything to offer Him, in my own state of spiritual brokenness, He loved and longed for me. I was wanted. I was seen. Just as my little girl was wanted, seen, and loved for all of who she was and all of who she was not. What unconditional, overwhelming love! What a taste of the Father's explosion of love for His creation in these still, small moments where my heart was bursting with love for this little broken girl.

Our pastor took her in his arms, and together in front of everyone there, we dedicated her to Jesus. She was His, always His, we had surrendered her to Him in the womb, and now we would do it again with her in our arms.

Once again, we often anticipate only the pain when we're asked to walk a journey beyond our comprehension; it's hard to imagine how love and joy can erupt too. It's hard to imagine that all the hardship we've walked through is worth it. It's hard to imagine that every last drop of pain we've walked through this side of heaven will one day be redeemed. All of it. Seeing Sophie gave me a small picture of that redemption, even amid all of the brokenness still surrounding me.

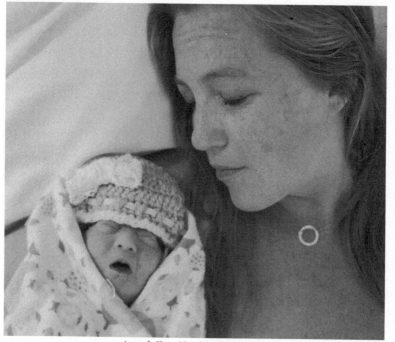

Amanda Kern, Now I Lay Me Down to Sleep Volunteer Photographer

It happened so fast, but I knew in that moment when God attuned my ears to the single lyric "newborn," that God had spoken. I didn't know how or what, but I tucked that word *newborn* that I had heard in my heart to find where it had come from later as I joyfully welcomed my sweet and lively little girl, Sophie, into my arms.

They brought her to us as fast as they could, Kevin holding her in his arms as I leaned my head over in awe of this sweet little one. I rubbed her chest, her cheeks with my fingers and nuzzled my face into hers as best as I could. Slowly, she started to move more, letting out the cutest little cries as if telling us she knew we were there. Ten of our family and friends crammed into the four-person viewing room behind us, loving her from afar. You would not have thought in that room that we knew we would lose her, our joy in just holding her overtaking our entire being. "She's here, she's here, she's here," I kept saying in quiet whispers, releasing all the tension, all the wondering, all the anxiety.

We had let God write her story, to give her life and breathe for however long He would choose. We wanted to know the end of His story for her here, and now we would. And we would enjoy her, care for her, and love her until the end of the story God had written for her on this earth and the beginning of her story for eternity began.

❀❀❀

I held her close to my chest, skin to skin, as they wheeled me out, and another song caught my ears as we moved through the hallway. My friends and family outside the doors to the operating room heard it too. It was the song "Happy Day" by Hillsong, and it speaks to the greatest coming day when death is defeated—the day when we stand "free at last" meeting Jesus face-to-face and "earthly pain finally will cease." And the song itself declares the reason for all of this—that the grave is no longer empty, and Jesus is alive. The experience of the nearness of God could not have been more palpable. His hand was even on the music that would play in such intimate moments of our time with Sophie. What a happy day it was! We got to hold and meet our daughter and were pointed over and over to the greatest Hope, the greatest promise we have—seeing Jesus face-to-face.

The promise. That song, the only word—*newborn*—that I heard. I wanted to know what that song was. Holding Sophie in our arms back in our recovery room, through disoriented and loopy words, I kept asking Kevin, "Did you hear the song? Did you hear the song?" No, he hadn't, and he must have thought I was just being delusional. So I stopped asking (but I promise, I will come back to this song soon) and just enjoyed Sophie, who had just been given her first little sponge bath by her daddy and now was safely swaddled in the blanket my mom had made for her. A little white crocheted hat, with a pink crochet flower I had made, covered her head. She looked so beautiful.

Amanda Kern, Now I Lay Me Down to Sleep Volunteer Photographer

A doctor from our church who specialized in comfort care for children was given last-minute permission to be at our side at the hospital. His watchful eyes, monitoring how Sophie was doing, comforted us and gave us freedom to just enjoy her even amid all of my anxiety-laden questions: "Is this OK? Is she OK? Can I hold her this way? What's that sound?"

Sophie seemed to do well snuggled in her blanket, quietly sleeping while lying next to me. So we invited our family into the room. We wanted her to experience the love of as many friends and family as possible, and we wanted to have a birthday party for her.

One by one our friends and family eagerly made their way into our hospital room. Kevin's parents walked through the doors first, his dad looking at me with tenderness, shaking his son's hand with pride and looking with love at his newest granddaughter. My parents, my brothers and sister, brother-in-law and nephews, best friends, and pastor all came in with joy written on their faces as they looked at this sweet little life. By the time everyone filed in the room, over twenty people surrounded my hospital bed.

We wanted to give our parents, family, and friends a chance to hold her. I loved watching them look at her with such tender love—a love made all the more powerful by the pain I could see in their eyes, as they knew this might be the only moment she would be in their arms alive. The collision of joy and pain crept back in as the reality of what was coming made its way back into my mind and heart.

Our pastor took her in his arms, and together in front of everyone there, we dedicated her to Jesus. She was His, always His, we had surrendered her to Him in the womb, and now we would do it again with her in our arms. And then we celebrated. I had asked my friend, Jennafer, the one who organized the secret Facebook group and weekly celebrations, to bring a cake full of sprinkles. She did not disappoint. And it was not just any cake, but a cake from the same place that Kevin and I had purchased our wedding cake.

Jennafer brought this beautiful cake covered with sprinkles and decorated with ten cherries encircling the top. Ten. A number that would become significant to us. Kevin took a cherry off and pretended to give it to Sophie, much to my dismay, and we all sang "Happy Birthday." I sang through tears, joyful that I could sing it to her with her in my arms. But also filled with the sorrow that it would be the first and last time I would sing it to her with her in my arms. We Facetimed our family and friends who could not be there and just enjoyed being with Sophie.

Sophie had come into the world at 12:28 a.m. on September 1, 2013, and I had not slept in two days. I wanted so badly to stay awake and enjoy every moment with her, but I struggled to keep my eyes open. Eventually as family and friends left, and our photos were taken, I succumbed to sleep; Sophie nestled in my right arm. I was content, sleeping with my daughter at my side, knowing my husband would keep a watchful eye over Sophie and wake me up soon. I only wished the soon would not have been so near the end.

# TWELVE

## The Best Is Yet to Come

*And life is just a vapor,*
*but God has said the best is yet to come.*

—The Joy Eternal, "The Best Is Yet
to Come"

I slowly woke up and saw in the shadow of the early dawn light seeping through the windows the silhouette of Kevin. He was holding Sophie, looking at her, and softly singing his favorite song, "Baby Mine," from the movie *Dumbo*. The words are a sweet picture of love in the midst of all the imperfections that are seen. It is one of his favorite songs, and one he was so looking forward to singing to his first daughter. He was rocking her gently as he whispered through tears the final words: "But, you're so precious to me, Sweet as can be, baby of mine."

I still cry when I hear him sing those words.

He quickly came over as he noticed me waking up.

"I think she's struggling a bit," he said.

We held onto each other, tears streaming down both of our faces, knowing the time to say goodbye was coming all too soon.

> I had never known what it really meant that
> Jesus bore our sorrow until those moments.

Because Sophie's brain had not formed, her ability to breathe was hindered. For Sophie, she would simply forget to breathe. Kevin noticed this before I did. And he constantly watched her, noticing when the time between her breaths became longer and longer. My sister, Laurie, couldn't bring herself to leave the hospital that night and spent the night in the chapel. She had told Kevin she would be there if we needed her. We quickly called her and asked her to come.

For the next few hours, it was just Kevin and me, my sister, and occasionally a nurse—reading to Sophie, loving on her, and crying with her.

With Kevin sitting next to me, Sophie between us, we pulled out the notes we had each written to her and read them through tears and overwhelming love as we held her and caressed her soft cheeks. We read to her *On the Night You Were Born* and wondered at the words "Heaven blew every trumpet and played every horn on the wonderful, marvelous night you were born."[1] What celebration her life had been, what glory her little quiet life had given our King. What was the audience of heaven thinking and feeling about her coming arrival, her life that spoke so loudly with no words?

We sat there, and we prayed and gave her to Jesus as we saw her strength fading, "You can go, sweet little girl," I said, though my heart ached inside of me. But as we read to her and rubbed her chest, she regained new strength and stayed a little while longer. She did this twice more, over the course of a couple of hours, causing us to laugh in the middle of our tears when laughter seemed so inappropriate. But Sophie was stubborn and our little fighter.

The third time, ten hours after she drew her first breath, my beautiful firstborn daughter drew her last breath peacefully, and with a soft smile on her lips she entered the presence of our King and now hers.

God's presence was so very near to us in those moments though the tears flowed freely and the ache was so deep. He was in our tears. He was in our ache. Jesus, the man of sorrows, was entering the sorrow of our loss. I had never known what it really meant that Jesus bore our sorrow until those moments.

※※※

My sister tenderly helped get prints of her feet and hands. I had brought my Bible and opened it to Isaiah 25, where it says, "And it will be said in that day, 'Behold, this is our God for whom we have waited that He might save us. This is the LORD for whom we have waited; Let us rejoice and be glad in His salvation'" (Isaiah 25:9). This is the verse that had been the prayer of my heart that I would wait for the Lord first as I waited for a husband. The verse that now is inscribed on my husband's wedding band. The verse that I noticed just a few weeks earlier is preceded by the following promise: "He will swallow up death for all time, And the Lord GOD will wipe tears away from all faces, And He will remove the reproach of His people for all the earth; For the LORD has spoken" (Isaiah 25:8). Perhaps I should have read the whole chapter before I made it one of my life verses, not knowing what surrounded that one verse would become such important truths for us to cling to. That verse is where I wanted to put her footprint. A reminder that it is the Lord we wait for and one day He will make all this broken pain whole.

---

We had so hoped we could bring her home,
but that was another sovereign no that we
could not comprehend.

---

I didn't want to let her go as we cared for her body and put the bright pink gingham dress, that included lace from my wedding dress, on her. Her

Mammo and Nini had made this dress with so much love. I had hoped it would be the outfit we brought her home in. Instead it was the outfit she would be buried in. She looked so beautiful in it. As we cried and held her little lifeless body, I wanted to find the song that played as she was pulled from my womb.

We scrolled through her playlist and found it—the title "The Best Is Yet to Come" by The Joy Eternal. You can hear on the audio that was recorded from her delivery the lyrics, "The labor pain that brings forth the newborn" and then you hear our doctor say, "She's here," right after. The timing of those words was astounding. Only God could have orchestrated such a moment from a playlist that was on "shuffle" and attune my ears to those words. What was this song talking about, "The Best Is Yet to Come?" The Best that is yet to come is His return when He makes all things new. This was the promise slowly being renewed and rooted in our hearts. This is what that entire song was talking about.

John Piper says:

> The life of the Godly is not a straight line to glory, but they do get there—God sees to it....Jesus points forward to the resurrection of our mortal bodies (Romans 8:23) when "death will be no more, neither shall there be mourning nor crying nor pain any more, for the former things have passed away" (Revelation 21:4). The best is yet to come. That is the unshakable truth about the life of the woman and the man who follow Christ in obedience of faith.[2]

Sophie's shell of a body was in our arms as we listened to the lyrics of the song pointing our eyes to Jesus, to eternity, and to a hope beyond the grave. I could not believe in the very moment our hearts were shaken to its core, grieving the loss of our daughter, that God had led us to this song of hope.

> I couldn't see with clarity in the midst of my grief how God was the Redeemer of even this pain. But I knew He was worthy even if my circumstance made little sense. And, oh, how I wanted to trust Him.

How would I say goodbye to her?

How could I endure life without her?

"Look up." Jesus was using this song to say to my heart.

Quietly, softly, gently, God was not asking me to have the strength to look up on my own, but provided music, people, events, and most importantly His Word, in order to put me in a place where all I could do was look up and see Him.

My sister left the room soon after, meeting my family through blurry eyes and telling them the news of Sophie's death. Everyone was surprised. When the family left in the wee hours of the morning, she was doing so well. Her color was a beautiful healthy pink, and she showed no signs of struggling to breathe.

❖❖❖

We had so hoped we could bring her home, but that was another sovereign no that we could not comprehend. Our family gathered into the room that we had been moved to on the other side of the hospital. The windows covering two walls gave way to a small view of the steeple of the chapel that Kevin and I had been married in just fourteen months before; the place that had been filled with so much hope and joy for the future; the place we had said our vows "and we'll serve our family and the world with the gospel of Jesus Christ"; the place we had lifted our hands and sung "How Great Is Our God." That place was within walking distance, and we could see it from the hospital room where we would say goodbye to our firstborn daughter.

As our family, a few friends, and pastor crowded into the room, with me holding Sophie, I knew I wanted to sing that song. The song we had sung as I walked down the aisle to my husband was the song I wanted to sing as we said goodbye to Sophie. For hadn't I chosen that song for our wedding for the picture it was of the true wedding feast? As a reminder that marriage is a picture, albeit a broken picture in this world, of the wedding feast we long for, where we are united with our Savior forever. And Sophie, our little sweet girl, had gotten to experience that picture become a reality before all of us. And so, after our pastor spoke a few words of the hope of heaven, we sang through tears once again, "How Great Is Our God."

I whispered the words "and time is in His hand, beginning and the end . . ." to my little girl and thought of how all would see and had seen how great our God was through her short life. It was a brutal and yet a holy moment of worship.

By this point, hundreds of thousands of people had been following our story in our community and online. Women had chosen life for their children through Sophie's story. People had told me stories of friends who had committed their lives to Jesus through Sophie's life, and friends had told me of how our journey had led them to a new surrender and trust in the Lord.

---

It is only because of Jesus that this is a story of hope, of victory, of things being restored that we have longed for, of good ultimately prevailing, and our hearts being able to rest with peace.

---

All of this seemed so worth it and not worth it all at once.

I couldn't help but think of how delighted Sophie must be in the presence of Jesus knowing how her little life had had an impact for Him. And yet I would have traded it all in that moment to have her alive with me.

I couldn't see with clarity in the midst of my grief how God was the Redeemer of even this pain. But I knew He was worthy even if my circumstance made little sense. And, oh, how I wanted to trust Him. He would have to cling to me because in these raw moments of grief I had no energy to cling to Him.

※※※

At 10:45 a.m., Sophie went to be with Jesus. God had given us ten precious hours with her, and they were indeed precious. Saying goodbye to her in that hospital room with family and friends was both a holy and brutal moment. Perhaps that is a taste of what the cross was like for Jesus, holy and brutal all at once. Sophie's life pointed our hearts to Jesus in a way we had never known.

As I was cleared to go home, Kevin wheeled me out of the hospital in what felt like one of the longest and loneliest journeys of my life, though family and friends surrounded us. My head held down, the little bear containing her heartbeat in one arm and another bear that was weighted, given to me as a gift from my nurse, Doreen, who had also lost two children, in my other hand, we made our way to our car just outside the hospital. Our car, now filled with our luggage, gifts for Sophie, blankets we had brought for her, balloons celebrating her arrival. But not Sophie.

It all felt so empty, so lonely, so quiet. Too quiet.

Kevin helped me up the flight of stairs to our apartment as I struggled to put one foot in front of the other, still in pain from my C-section. A new flood of emotion overtook me as I looked at our front door and said, "There is supposed to be a sign. A sign declaring, 'Welcome Home, Sophie.'" But there wasn't, because Sophie wasn't there.

The coming days were full of tears, a new season of grief, and a new perspective of our Savior as we begin to learn how to navigate our lives with the constant tension of the joy of knowing our little girl fully and the sorrow of her absence from our lives. It was often hard to step outside of myself and think not just of what I was feeling but of the impact of Sophie's life and what she was now experiencing. Kevin put to words so much of the fresh perspective God was writing on our hearts in this new season of grief just a few days after Sophie's death:

As we grieve and celebrate together, I'm getting to see certain things—even things that used to seem so familiar—in a new light. Two days ago I spent time with God, listening and talking with Him. I wrote in my journal some of what I was processing, and these are some words I wrote as I listened to the song "The Best Is Yet to Come," that was playing when Sophie was born . . .

Sophie's life has been about a lot of things, but there has been one resounding voice heard above everything else. It has drawn in so many people, both those who have realized it and those who have not. Her life has pointed people to Jesus. It is only because of Jesus that this is a story of hope, of victory, of things being restored that we have longed for, of good ultimately prevailing, and our hearts being able to rest with peace. It's only because of Jesus that this is a story where we don't have to make up some comforting, yet make-believe thoughts to calm our hearts in order to get by. Because of Jesus we can stand firmly in the full reality of what is true and real and actual right now, and our hearts leap with enormous joy and celebration. Without Jesus this would be a very different story, especially now.

But thousands of years ago Jesus stepped into this story. Thousands of years ago Jesus stepped into everything that was messed up and horrible and wrong about this world and our lives. He stepped into the story of humanity that seemed to have gone horribly wrong. And Jesus began to set things right again. He began to lay His hands upon people and heal sickness, diseases, and death. He began to give people the love and acceptance they longed to experience but never realized they could fully find from God. He began to teach people how to give that same love to others in a new way, not from themselves, but from God. He began to forgive people as they realized they had rebelled against the One who was actually for them, God. And He pointed them back to lives focused on and surrendered to God.

And then He finished what He began. Jesus finished the great rescue plan that had been put in place by God ever since things began to go awry long ago. Jesus took the effects of brokenness, sickness, and death; He took the penalty of our rebellion; He took the consequences of our sin; He took the curse and Satan's ability to steal, and to kill, and to destroy. He took them all upon Himself on the cross. And then He died physically, emotionally, and spiritually. He was taken away from those who loved Him on this earth, and for the first time He was taken away from the One who had loved Him and been with Him for eternity, our God and His Father. Because He took on everything we should have carried ourselves, He experienced the full separation each of us should someday experience. But He took it all on so that we wouldn't have to.

And then once He had fully taken on all the horrible realities and nature of our lives and this world so that it was finished, complete, and sealed, Jesus came back to life. He conquered death, illness, rebellion, sin, brokenness, separation, the curse, and Satan's attempts to steal, kill, and destroy. And in that moment of Jesus' resurrection, He secured that everything would be restored. That everything that isn't as it was meant to be will be made untrue, and once again we would be reunited with our loving Father, God, and He would once again have total authority and control over our lives and all things—to bring it all back to how it was meant to be.

It's because of this—all Jesus is and all He did—that at the moment Sophie quietly passed out of our arms on Sunday, our prayers were finally answered. She was now healed and fully whole—illness no longer reigned. She was now fully alive—the sting of death was no longer a threat. She was now experiencing God's full love, care, and protection—the limitations of love on this earth were no longer hindrances. Our sweet daughter, Sophie, is now in a place that we know with assurance that we will be with her again soon because our trust is in Jesus. And while we are still on this earth and thus grieving her not being with us and grieving the realities of this world that aren't as God originally intended them to be, we know that just as Sophie's story finished with her life being restored back to the perfect, wonderful, and glorious way it was meant to be, the same Hero written into her story is written into ours. (Even if long ago you chose to have nothing to do with Jesus, in reading this now, He has stepped back into your story.) And if we place our trust in Jesus and allow Him to be the central hero of our story, we too will someday experience all things being set back to what they should be, just as our sweet Sophie is experiencing right now.

I honestly don't think I have ever loved Jesus like I do right at this moment. He rescued my little daughter's life . . . and I care about that even more than Him rescuing my own life.

Kevin's words reminded me afresh the best *is* yet to come. The redemption of all things.

Just a few days later as we sat by the gravesite, facing the unimaginable task of burying our firstborn daughter, we were reminded once again that the grave was not the end, that the anchor of our Hope was Jesus. And He was sure and steadfast during life's storms. Our hope was as fixed on eternity and the hope of heaven as we thought it could be that day.

# THIRTEEN

## The Other Shoe Drops

*Our challenge in dry and dark times is to respond in simple faith—
to believe that the unseen Divine Shepherd is with us in our unlit valley. We grope in hope until rays of light begin to push the night away.*

—Dr. Timothy S. Laniak

Four months after Sophie had passed away was the turn of a new year and the hope that this would be the year that would bring more joy than pain. My word for the year: Joy.

I had written in my journal at the beginning of the year the words of David from the Book of Psalms: "Weeping may last for the night, but a shout of joy comes in the morning" (Psalm 30:5b). I hoped that this would be the year we would get to bring home a little baby. I hoped God would continue to bring healing to my still-broken and grieving heart, and I hoped God would continue to point others to Jesus through the life of Sophie. I had my ideas of how God would unfold what that joy would be. But I had no idea how differently He would choose to answer my prayers for what I hoped 2014 would hold for our family, for me, for another child.

Two months into the new year, just six months after welcoming

Sophie into the world and saying goodbye, we were pregnant again. I was hopeful, and yet fear gripped my heart more easily this time.

I knew now that tragedy befalls us all, often unexpectedly, and I no longer was naïve to think it only happened to others. I understood tragedy could happen at any time and at any place. And though I recognized that God was in control, His sovereignty left me feeling less, not more, secure. I feared what tragedy He would ask us to endure next.

I wrestled with trusting God with the future of this baby as we waited the week we would be able to find out if this child carried the same condition as Sophie. The mere thought of walking through carrying another child who would not live induced near panic.

"I cannot walk through this again, God; do not make me do this again," I would often say with both a demanding and pleading spirit.

Doctors, nurses, friends would try to calm the fears with comments like, "We've never seen it happen twice" or "There's no reason to think it would happen again" or "I'm sure everything will be fine." I wanted to hold onto their words with hope. Yet I realized in the recesses of my heart that no one had the ability to make those kinds of guarantees.

A month before we would be able to find out whether this child was sick or healthy, the fear of walking through another loss overwhelmed me. But I stumbled across a small paragraph from a man named David Guthrie, who had lost two children, in a devotional I was reading. And his words struck me to the core:

"'I spent my life waiting for the other shoe to drop. The shoe has dropped. I had thought I was invulnerable. Now I know better. I thought, *Our child has died. How much worse can it get?* There's less to fear. God will be enough for us. Now we say it out of experience.'"[1]

Guthrie was speaking right to my heart in those moments. I was living in fear of the next shoe dropping. Ever since Sophie passed away my fear had been: "Lord, who will You take next? What's the next thing to drop in my life?" I didn't have that same confidence that Guthrie spoke of. My view of God had been both rooted deeper and shaken. I wanted things to go my way this time—or at least my idea of what would be fair and right and good.

My mind was fixated on fears of the future instead of living in the reality that His grace would be sufficient for me in whatever He asked me to walk through now, not later. I often forgot how God was enough for us as we walked through the life and death of our daughter, Sophie. Yet underneath all of my fears I was mostly confident that He would be enough for us in whatever He asked us to walk through next. I just didn't want there to be another "next" hard thing. Would I trust Him for today and not what I feared tomorrow would bring?

❁❁❁

This time, because of Sophie's condition, we went to our high-risk doctor earlier to find out our child's condition. With Sophie we found out at twenty weeks, but with our second baby we would have the ultrasound at twelve weeks pregnant, the earliest you can tell whether the brain and skull have begun to develop.

With nervous excitement, Kevin and I drove to Dr. A's office, the office we became so familiar with over the course of the last year, eager to hear a good report and celebrate with all the nurses, technicians, and our doctor.

We pulled out our camera and took a quick video before we headed into our appointment. As we sat in the car, phone in hand, we looked into the camera, and I said, "So, we're twelve weeks pregnant with you . . ."Kevin interrupts with joy, saying, "Hi, Little Baby," and said, "And we're about to go into the doctor with a super-high-powered ultrasound so we can see you and make sure that you are looking great and healthy and everything is forming including your brain and your skull. We're about to see you more up close and personal than we've gotten to see you before." I quickly said, "So we're really excited and nervous and hoping for a really good report." And as if I knew, through tears, added, "But whatever we find out we're going to love and celebrate you for as long as God gives us you."

I hadn't planned on saying that at the end.

Kevin turned off the video, we prayed, and we got out of our car. Holding hands tightly, we made our way up to the second floor, entering the doors marked "Fetal Diagnostic Center" for the umpteenth time, but it felt like the first. It had been over six months since we had been there and seen Dr. A and our sonographer, Robyn, both of whom we had become quite endeared to.

⊠⊠⊠

We sat in the waiting room, waiting somewhat patiently to be called back. We took countless deep breaths, assured each other that it would probably be fine, while both wondering in the quietness of our hearts if that would actually be true.

Robyn called me back, and we made friendly banter, catching up on the last several months as I settled into the chair and she started the ultrasound scan. She felt like a friend at this point after seeing her so often throughout our pregnancy with Sophie, and I was glad to see her again. I told her we were nervous and she smiled. I can't remember the rest of our conversation except that at some point as I watched this tiny little baby on the video monitor, Robyn grew silent. She didn't have a good poker face. I knew something was off, so I asked her if she could see the skull.

"Sometimes it's too hard to tell at this stage," she said not too convincingly.

She was looking for words we might believe to buy her time and not give her own emotions away. But I had been to enough ultrasounds that I knew those words weren't true.

I didn't push back, perhaps fearing what we might hear, and she left the room quickly. She had printed off photos, and Kevin and I stared intently at them trying to see if we could see a skull. We were now pretty good at looking at ultrasound video and photos and figuring out where the head and feet and butt were. So we could tell that something was off with our baby's head. It didn't quite look like Sophie's, but it also didn't look like the skull was fully there either.

Neither of us could bring ourselves to say the unimaginable. Silently I waited with Kevin, while the emotions inside of me rose in nervous fear. When the minutes dragged on, and no one came back in the room, our fear only grew.

> Of course I knew this could happen, but I didn't truly think God would ask us to walk the same journey. Twice.

Was I about to face my worst nightmare, again?

God seemed as distant as He could be in that moment. There was no peace and no calm in that room, only fear. Dr. A, who had become like family to us over the previous year, finally came into the room. He took the little wand, putting the warm jelly back on my belly, looked at our little baby, reached for my hand, and with pain in his own eyes said, "It's not anencephaly."

A short-lived breath of relief.

"It's called acrania. It's where the brain has formed but the skull has not and will not. But it plays out the same as anencephaly."

An eruption of the kind of wailing grief that comes when you have just found out that someone has died suddenly rose out of both Kevin and me. And though our little baby was still alive, this child would die, and it felt like death to us. This was not only a death of a child we were anticipating but the ever-slow realization of the death of our dreams for having a biological child, for how our family would form.

Dr. A tenderly held my hand and told us we could go to a different room when we were ready and he'd like to come talk with us. I found out later that they had waited so long to come into our room because no one knew how they would tell us we would walk this journey again. They knew we would choose life, so Dr. A didn't even tell us our options but valued this little life and our decision to carry our child to term once again.

It seemed the entire office was grieving with us. It felt like too much, and even as I think of those moments a knot forms in my stomach, for I have no idea how we endured that news—much less the weeks and months that followed—apart from the grace of God.

That grace that seemed so far and distant in that moment was still there, though this time unseen.

All the reserves we had going into our journey with Sophie had been depleted. We were coming out of the heaviness of that season of deep grief but still tired and weary and still grieving. It felt as if all of my categories for who God was and how He worked were shaken to the core for the first time. Of course I knew this could happen, but I didn't truly think God would ask us to walk the same journey. Twice.

---

It felt as if God was teasing us with the joy and hope of new life, only to be crushed with the reality that we were going back into a valley of loss that felt more like the valley of the shadow of death this time.

---

How could He? How could He allow us to not only lose another baby, but to have to endure losing this baby the exact same way we lost Sophie? If He was going to ask us to suffer again, why not be a little more creative?

Julie, my best friend, and Laurie, my sister, were both pregnant, and this was supposed to be a year of joy, a year of redemptive joy. I would not only lose my child but also watch the closest people in my life have healthy children. It seemed cruel and unkind.

It seemed so unfair.

> I like things to be fair. The other shoe was supposed to stay on. I looked around me and saw no one else walking through such pain. I saw healthy pregnancies and growing happy families. Why were we chosen again for tragedy?

*Are you a cruel, unkind, and unfair God?* I wondered, as I tried to make sense of His ways in these brutal moments.

❖❖❖

We sat in the car in shock, in a daze, and yet I knew we had to find a way to worship God in spite of everything inside of me that felt as if He had just abandoned me. I had recently heard a song entitled "Though You Slay Me" by Shane and Shane, where they put to music words first spoken by a man named Job and the prophet Hosea.

The lyrics "Though you slay me, yet I will praise you" are a reflection of Job's heart after he suffered immeasurable loss, unsure of how or why. But Job knew God in such a way that he would continue to praise God in the midst of his own unanswered questions. "The LORD gave, and the LORD has taken away; blessed be the name of the LORD" (Job 1:21 ESV). Job speaks these words in the excruciating aftermath of the loss of much of his family, home, and livelihood. I understood these words for the first time in my own raw pain, and they were words of my own declaration of worship amid all the questions of what had just unfolded. So we listened to that song by Shane and Shane in the car as confusion and angst riddled our bodies.

And surprising peace came for the first time in the midst of our shattered hearts in those moments. And it came as we worshipped in faith. Not because we felt like worshipping but because we knew God was still worthy. I knew my human mind was not capable of understanding what

God understood about our circumstances. And I knew somewhere in our pain that He was still there. It was completely different from how we experienced finding out Sophie's condition.

It was so much darker.

We did what we had done when we found out Sophie's condition and drove to Julie's house, said the same words, "Our baby won't live," and I crumbled into her arms. I remember at some point saying, "I want to fight for our friendship; I don't want this to come between us," knowing her growing healthy baby would be due just a month after mine. How could this not tear us apart? The pain . . . the jealousy. New things we would engage in together, trust the Lord with together, and fight for together.

It felt as if God was teasing us with the joy and hope of new life, only to be crushed with the reality that we were going back into a valley of loss that felt more like the valley of the shadow of death this time. *Surely this is not the way to know You, God? Surely this is not the way to the joy and hope I was longing for this year?*

⊗⊗⊗

Once again, I felt like Much-Afraid, from Hurnard's book, on her own journey to the high places. In a scene where she had just come out of a valley to get a glimpse of the glorious high places she was headed to, she realizes that she must go down once again to go up. And the place she was to go was the "Valley of Loss." The Shepherd appears to her as she considers turning back altogether.

> He lifted her up, supported her by his arm, and with his own hand wiped the tears from her cheeks, then said in his strong, cheery voice, "There is no question of your turning back, Much-Afraid. No one, not even your own shrinking heart, can pluck you out of my hand. Don't you remember what I told you before? 'This delay is not unto death but for the glory of God.' . . . Will you bear this too,

> Much-Afraid? Will you suffer yourself to lose or to be
> deprived of all that you have gained on this journey to the
> High Places? Will you go down . . . into the Valley of Loss,
> just because it is the way that I have chosen for you? Will
> you still trust and still love me?"[2]

Would I still trust Him and say yes to Him, even if it meant walking into the valley of the shadow of death, the valley of loss, once again? I like things to be fair. The other shoe was supposed to stay on. I looked around me and saw no one else walking through such pain. I saw healthy pregnancies and growing happy families. Why were we chosen again for tragedy? Everyone else "appeared" to have both shoes securely tied to their feet.

---

He took on the grief and sorrow and sin of
this world and then crushed all of its power
with His resurrection power so we could
know Him and spend eternity with Him free
from the pain of this world and the grip
of death in our own lives.

---

"Why? Why us and not them? Why them and not us? Why is life so incredibly unfair at times?"

These were the questions that shook me as I wrestled deeply those first few weeks of settling into another journey of pain and sorrow. But soon I began to notice stories all around me of pain. And I began seeing them in a different light than I had before, reminding me in all the questions running through my own mind, that I do not live in a world of fairness.

I was not the only one who had experienced the unfairness of life, the sheer seemingly "randomness" of tragedy and pain. Most of the world knows life can be so unfair. And there is One who suffered the greatest unfairness of all: Jesus.

How could God be so kind to me and so unfair to Himself? The penalty for our wrong is death. (See Romans 6:23.) But Jesus came and took the form of man, not counting equality with God a thing to be grasped. He laid His life down, taking on every wrong ever committed in this world—past, present, and future—and paid for it so that we could have life; so that we could have the promise of a future with Him now and for eternity.

I didn't deserve that. I absolutely knew I didn't deserve that. It wasn't fair that He, total perfection, should take on my sins, that I could have life. The questions I had for God were many, but God was reminding me through His Spirit that He suffered unfairness too. He went the way that most would say, "This cannot be the way," and He did so willingly, sacrificially, and because of His great love for me.

The weight of the cross became more illuminated for me in this season of deep darkness.

---

I imagine if life were about how we define fairness, Jesus would never have come to pay the debt we had no ability to pay ourselves.

---

When I couldn't understand my suffering or the suffering of this world, I knew Jesus didn't just turn a blind eye to our suffering. He entered the suffering and suffered with us.

"He was despised and rejected by men, a man of sorrows and acquainted with grief; . . . Surely he has borne our griefs and carried our sorrows" (Isaiah 53:3-4 ESV).

And in His suffering there was a promise—a promise of total redemption to come, and a promise of redemption *in* the suffering because He didn't stay dead. He took on the grief and sorrow and sin of this world and then crushed all of its power with His resurrection power so we could know Him and spend eternity with Him free from the pain of this world and the grip of death in our own lives. "In this world you will have trouble. But take heart! I have overcome the world" (John 16:33 NIV).

God's power was redeeming our lives with Sophie's story; we saw it and we experienced it. What should have been only a story of pain and death and heartache had become a story where the threads of hope and joy and life weaved their way in and through the heartache. His power to redeem *in* the suffering was written all over Sophie's story. And so Kevin and I, in the midst of our devastation, were continuing to be reminded that Jesus would still restore and redeem all things, including this part of our story that appeared broken beyond repair.

> "'He will wipe every tear from their eyes. There will be no more death' or mourning or crying or pain, for the old order of things has passed away." He who was seated on the throne said, "I am making everything new!" Then he said, "Write this down, for these words are trustworthy and true." (Revelation 21:4-5 NIV)

Even though it felt as though all of our hopes and dreams had been washed away, the best was still yet to come.

I didn't know how God would give us glimpses of redemption with this child; the path ahead was more than daunting. But we had seen Him do it before, and we knew He would do it again. So as I continued to experience the agonizing confusion and questions of how could this be happening again, I began to let those emotions I felt give me a taste of what it's like to respond to the grace of the free gift of love and sacrifice that came to me on the cross through Jesus. Oh, how could He die for me to give me life? How could He take on all the pain in this world so that we could live in freedom?

It. Is. So. Unfair.

It surely didn't answer the questions of why God allows what He does (you could read a thousand other books on that topic alone). But it did move my heart to be unable to shake His love for me in those shocking and painful moments where His love appeared distant and my circumstances did not reflect my idea of a loving God.

I imagine if life were about how we define fairness, Jesus would never have come to pay the debt we had no ability to pay ourselves. And I wouldn't have life or freedom or even an inkling of hope that there is redemption in this story now and to come. Jesus is the only One that offers hope and redemption *in* the suffering and one day freedom *from* the suffering. So, really, Jesus was the only One that made a whole lot of sense to me in those initial days and weeks following our second child's diagnosis.

As my heart clung more tightly to Jesus, I was beginning to catch glimpses of how His hope would be forged in our hearts, not only through the waiting for a child but also in our suffering. Sophie's story felt like a taste of suffering, but this journey was a journey through the very heart of suffering. I didn't know I could feel more pain than what I felt with losing Sophie, but the weight of the sorrow was unlike anything I had experienced in the previous year.

And though our journey with Dasah would end the same as with Sophie, her journey and her story would be strikingly different.

The other shoe had dropped, and now I would see how faithful and good God really was and discover a joy based not on circumstance but on His presence alone.

# FOURTEEN

## The Invitation in Our Suffering

*Shall we scorn that God has revealed so little concerning His ways, or rejoice that He has revealed so much?*

—Gene Edwards

Just nine months after Sophie had died, we found out our second child would not live. And though we still were grieving the deep loss of Sophie, her story seemed almost easy compared to the one we now had entered. It didn't help that it had been just a few days before our second anniversary when our dreams were crushed once again.

Two years—we had only been married two years and walked through such tragedy in our young marriage.

We went away that weekend—a trip to the Gulf Coast in Florida that we had planned months before, not knowing the atmosphere that trip would have. The trip was now clouded with pain in the midst of celebrating our young marriage.

I wondered how we would survive this time. Would people still come alongside of us? How could we ask them to bear such a burden with us again? Who would meet us in the darkness and sit with us in this astounding pain?

My friend Elizabeth, who had helped me grow in my faith in college, sent me a song I listened to on repeat that week. Music was a constant companion for me to help lift my eyes to Jesus in the moments where I could hardly open my Bible, and where my confident hope in Jesus would so quickly be lost in a sea of despair. Elizabeth had sent me the song "Sovereign Over Us" by Michael W. Smith. The lines reached to the depths of my ravaged soul and reminded me that God was with us in our sorrow.

That weekend as I listened to that song on repeat, I clung to the words at the end of the song: "Your plans are still to prosper, you have not forgotten us." What unseen plan was being played out in this broken story, where it felt as though God had forgotten us?

Kevin and I took our chairs out to a quiet beach, talked, cried, and just stared at the vastness of the ocean before us. Eventually we took out a large piece of paper to record our memories from our second year of marriage. It's a tradition we began just a year before, a way for us to remember what God had done, the memories we had made, and the things we didn't want to forget.

---

I was overwhelmed in that moment and thankful for the ways God was continuing to use His Spirit in His people to reveal what we needed, when we needed it, and not a moment sooner.

---

We wrote in bullet points, not even short sentences, all the ways we had celebrated with Sophie's life and seen God show up. Even in our grief we looked at each other, the ocean before us, the wind on our faces, and said with smiles and unexpected words, "It's been a good year, a rich year."

It was good to remember and to see how after walking through such a painful journey we could say, "It's been good." It wasn't good because we felt everything in it had been good. We could say, "It's been good," because

God's presence had been with us in the midst of all the hard and painful turns. It was good to remember His provision in the midst of all the pain. And it was what we needed to remember as we anticipated what year three of our marriage would hold.

Would we look back and say, "It's been a good year" again? Would God show up in the same ways He showed up before? Would He be near or far? How would this death of our second child affect our marriage? Our friendships? So many questions, but that day there was hope. Hope that the same God who held us through our journey with Sophie, and for so many previous years, would show up in this new journey with our second child.

It would be different (this child was different); how we walked into this journey was different; and yet our God was the same—yesterday, today, and forever.

God spoke these truths through the prophet of Isaiah when He said: "Even to your old age I will be the same, And even to your graying years I will bear you!" (Isaiah 46:4). When it didn't feel as though He was or would be the same God, we clung to what we knew was true, what His unchanging Word says about His unchanging character and ways.

⊗⊗⊗

One week after finding out our child's condition, Jennafer once again came alongside of our family and asked to come over with another new friend, Holly. I was so weary; the mere thought of celebrating in the extravagant ways we did with Sophie was overwhelming. Neither Kevin nor I really knew what we even needed.

Holly and Jennafer made their way into our small apartment holding a black rectangular vintage-looking mailbox. They knelt in front of us and shared how they had been praying about what we needed and how they could come alongside us in this journey. One of the things they wanted to do was to remind us we didn't have to walk this journey alone.

One of my questions had been: "Who would want to walk this journey with us once, much less twice?" and gratitude filled my heart as they spoke into those unspoken fears.

They then presented us the mailbox. On the front, it said, "For this child we have prayed . . ." a verse from 1 Samuel 1:27. And on the back it said, "Love, your Supporting C.A.S.T.," with the words "Come Along Side Them" written next to those capitalized letters.

They opened this beautiful mailbox to reveal a stack of colorful envelopes with upcoming dates on them. They told us that this was the first of many letters to come; a letter every day to encourage us on this journey and remind us we were not alone. From that day on, until Dasah's birth, we had colorful envelopes filling that box with notes from friends, family, and strangers breathing hope and life into our weary hearts. It sits on our bookshelf, filled to the brim with cards, to this day. I was overwhelmed in that moment and thankful for the ways God was continuing to use His Spirit in His people to reveal what we needed, when we needed it, and not a moment sooner.

One desire we expressed to them was to experience the more fun and "normal" things of pregnancy that we didn't get to experience with Sophie. Like a shower or gender reveal. We wanted to establish some normalcy and some different memories this time.

We had not found out the gender of this baby yet, so we decided that one way we wanted to invite community into our little growing baby's story was to have a gender reveal party.

Jennafer, Holly, and Elyse took on this feat. And what of course in my mind was going to be quite simple turned into a gender reveal that would put to shame every gender reveal Pinterest board you've ever seen.

⁂

We found out a few days before our reveal the sex of our baby and knew we wanted to reveal it with paint and fun. We wanted everyone to show up in white T-shirts and spray them with the color of the gender!

That's all we knew would happen when we showed up to a little park next to a large lake in our white T-shirts with excited, yet heavy hearts.

*We're doing this again*, is all I could keep thinking. *We're celebrating another child that will not live.* "Oh, Lord, help us enjoy the day. Help me embrace the tears and the joy that come" was the prayer of my heart.

"Are you ready?" Jennafer said as she met us at our car to escort us to the pavilion. We said yes, shed some tears, and then walked toward our first gender reveal CARNIVAL—where we discovered they hadn't just taken over one pavilion but all of them.

---

We would welcome another little girl, we would celebrate her, and then we would say goodbye. Though the day was filled with the joy of celebrating this new life, heaviness loomed in our hearts as we ate cake and talked with friends covered from head to toe in pink paint.

---

We saw a woman on stilts dressed from head to toe in an eccentric pink-and-blue outfit.

A stilt walker. There was a stilt walker at our party.

A pretty hat sat sideways on her head filled with pink and blue bows. Ridiculously large pink and blue yarn balls hung around her neck, and pink and blue gingham material flowed from her waist (think *Gone with the Wind*). Large palazzo-style pants followed the billows cascading from her waist around her hips down to the ground. Elyse, my friend with close connections with the Princess Aurora, had skillfully sewn her outfit.

A sign welcomed everyone, saying, "Welcome to Baby Dennis's Carnival." We then walked under a large homemade banner that said "Pink or Blue" in their respective colors.

Inside the first pavilion, our friend Carrie, who had presented us with

Sophie's cute yellow tutu on my belly for our magical day at Disney, was getting the cotton candy machine ready. There was a beautiful cake, and countless little blue and pink details were scattered throughout (from the cups to the straws and plates).

---

In the midst of our grief, and our wondering if people would continue to rally around us, we were reminded over and over that our family and friends were with us. And they would celebrate this little girl once again and love her for as long as God would give her to us.

---

Jennafer walked me to another pavilion that had a backdrop for a photo booth, and then another where a friend who did professional face painting would paint our cheeks—or whatever we wanted painted. She then led us to the table that meant the most to us: on it was a map of the United States created on a corkboard with gold pins set to the side, made by Elyse.

Throughout the evening, friends would pray for us and call other friends to pray. Pins were placed all over the map, wherever prayers were coming from. As it hit social media, more and more people began to pray. Soon we realized that perhaps Elyse should have created a map of the whole world! By the end of the week we put hundreds of pins in the map—not only in the United States but across the world representing people "Coming Along Side" of us in prayer and joining our Supporting C.A.S.T.

We gathered everyone, all forty friends who had shown up, and lined up ten phones on four music stands to video call our family and friends who couldn't be there to see the big reveal. We had told no one the sex of our child. Our friends, Brandon and Mac, had been recording the party the entire time and positioned themselves to try to miss getting hit by paint and capture the moment when everyone would know who this little child was and who they would celebrate and say goodbye to. It was hard to think of the goodbye part in that moment, everything was so celebratory. But it was in the back of my mind, and that thought wasn't lost on me—as there would soon be an eruption of joy at the news, and sorrow too.

Everyone turned around as Kevin and I stood in front of a pink bucket filled with pink paint and a blue one filled with blue paint. Pink and blue balloons had been filled with their respective paint colors to be used once the spray of color began. We counted down, and Kevin and I teased those who were recording as we placed our color guns in the blue and then the pink until we pulled the pink paint back into our guns, releasing it on the countdown of three. A spray of pink paint flew far out of our paint guns at everyone as they turned around, and our typically more-chill friend, Kristel, jumped into the sky screaming, "It's a girl!"

---

It was an invitation once again, an invitation
for others and for us. An invitation for
others to come alongside of us and learn
what it looked like to journey through
suffering with another.

---

Chaos ensued, and soon the joy and excitement of paint spray, water balloons, and silly string were coming from all angles. By the end we looked like we had just completed a color run. But it was just a gender reveal.

Our family watched with joy and tears.

We would welcome another little girl, we would celebrate her, and then we would say goodbye. Though the day was filled with the joy of celebrating this new life, for she was indeed worth celebrating, heaviness loomed in our hearts as we ate cake and talked with friends covered from head to toe in pink paint.

※※※

My parents and siblings who were scattered across the country couldn't be there that day so a few days later, my youngest brother, Dan, sent me a photo of him in New York's Central Park by himself, dousing himself with pink powder as he held a sign saying, "Celebrating Sophie has a sister." Not to be outdone, my parents, sister, brother-in-law, and nephews all put on white shirts and took a video of themselves, too, in a pink paint fight. And then my brother Luke, who worked at a camp, sent me this message:

> So yesterday a little surprise took place here at Kivu. After your gender reveal and Dan's goofy picture in the park of celebrating your baby girl, I ordered 25 lbs. of pink powder so we could also celebrate here. However, after ordering the powder, I asked our leadership staff to help me celebrate . . . and here's what they surprised me with yesterday before lunch! Hope you enjoy! This is for you guys and my newest niece!

Luke's staff had gathered the hundreds of students and staff into their large gym, a huge banner of celebration on the wall. They greeted Luke when he came in with pounds and pounds of pink powder flying through the air, everyone shouting, "It's a girl." The video Luke sent included not only that celebration but also messages from young kids at the camp of how our little girl's life was already impacting theirs.

In the midst of our grief, and our wondering if people would continue to rally around us, we were reminded over and over that our family and friends were with us. And they would celebrate this little girl once again and love her for as long as God would give her to us.

❖❖❖

Instead of weekly celebrations, we decided to do weekly family times. Again, we wanted to establish some normalcy to this journey. We wanted to start traditions we would do as a family if our daughter would be here with us, not knowing if we would ever get to have a child in our arms to parent that would live.

I loved doing simple things like family movie nights, getting Popsicles at a local shop, and playing games. And I was so proud to take her (and Kevin) to her first Ohio State Buckeyes game (my family is a bit obsessed). Close family and friends threw us showers where they gifted us with things that would give us respite and covered us in prayer. We took our first family vacation and went out west, road tripping up the California coast and meeting Kevin's extended family for a reunion in the fields of Yosemite.

In all the sweet memories we would make with her, the darkness of our journey produced a heavy and lonely weight upon my heart. What did God have for this little girl, and what was He doing in this strange and backward story I felt He was writing for us?

It was an invitation once again, an invitation for others and for us. An invitation for others to come alongside of us and learn what it looked like to journey through suffering with another. And an invitation for us to wrestle afresh with God, continuing to peel back the layers of our heart that had built a faulty view of Him and see Him replace those layers with deeper truth and a more steadfast understanding of Hope.

# FIFTEEN

## THE MYRTLE TREE

*And instead of a thorn now, the cypress towers*
*And instead of the briar the myrtle blooms with a thousand flowers.*

—Andrew Peterson, "The Sowers Song"

I n ancient Hebrew history there is a tree known for its resilience amid harsh weather. It's called a "myrtle tree" and originates in the oasis of the dry and arid climate of the Middle East.

In the Hebrew language, this tree goes by the name of Hadassah, translated in our English text as "Esther." In the Bible, Esther was a young Jewish woman, living in a time when her people were persecuted and lived in slavery. Called into the courts of the king to be presented as his wife, she obediently went. But when a plot arose by one of the king's sidekicks to destroy her people, the Jews, she faced a life or death decision: Go to the king on behalf of her people and plead for their lives at the risk of her own death for entering his presence without being summoned, or stay silent and watch her people perish.

The man who raised her admonished her with words of conviction: "For if you remain silent at this time, relief and deliverance will arise for the Jews from another place and you and your father's house will perish. And who knows whether you have not attained royalty for such a time as this?" (Esther 4:14).

---

> I did not think this companion of suffering, gripping my hand much more tightly than before, was leading me to God.

---

So Esther called upon her people to pray and fast, asking God for favor upon her as she entered the king's presence without being summoned. And in tremendous courage she declares, "and if I perish, I perish" (Esther 4:16).

She would count the cost to save her people even if it cost her very life. The king honored her request, and ultimately her people were spared destruction.

This has been a story of faith, courage, and deliverance I have always loved in the Bible. Esther is a picture of what it looks like to walk by faith and not by sight. She displayed such courage in a time when women held little power and their words held little weight. She trusted her God could give weight to her words and very life if He so chose. And she would offer herself willingly to be a vessel for His use, trusting that He had placed her in the courts of the king perhaps "for such a time as this," even amid her fears.

As Kevin and I prayed about the name for our second daughter, the phrase "for such a time as this" continued to surface in our hearts. I couldn't comprehend what God would have in store for our second daughter, but I believed He was setting the stage to produce something in and through our family's life that would bring great glory to God and His hope to many "for such a time as this."

I have always loved the Hebrew word for Esther, *Hadassah*. I didn't realize until we researched her name that it meant "myrtle tree." As I studied the significance of this tree, I learned that the branches of the myrtle tree were used during the Jewish Feast of Booths. This feast was one of the annual feasts and celebrations the Jewish people partook of where they would celebrate and remember God's presence with them in the wilderness. And, ultimately, this feast was a foreshadowing of the time when we would permanently dwell with Jesus!

I also discovered the flowers you find in bloom on the myrtle tree, though bitter to the taste, when crushed produce an aroma sweeter than a rose. It was my prayer that out of the bitterness of this journey the Lord would produce a sweet aroma that flowed out of my life and into the lives of others. I didn't know how He would do it. In the initial weeks following her diagnosis it all felt so very bitter, but I was beginning to trust God that in His time the sweet would rise.

The name Hadassah seemed a bit old for our little girl who would in many ways always be a little girl to us, and so we shortened Hadassah to Dasah, pronouncing it DAH-sa.

In keeping with Kevin's Irish heritage, we wanted a Gaelic name somewhere in there and so discovered the name Brielle. And like Sophie's middle name, Kyla, Brielle is both Gaelic and Hebrew. In Gaelic it simply means "Hill" and in Hebrew it means "God is our might." Surely, God is our might and the One, the only One who could produce life and joy and hope through the journey He had asked us to walk with our sweet Dasah Brielle Dennis.

Who knew but that God had chosen Dasah to enter our lives "for such a time as this"—perhaps to leave a sweeter aroma in our lives and those around us than we could even imagine and remind us in the wilderness of the hope we have in Christ's coming and His return.

⊠⊠⊠

Still, I thought walking through our journey with Sophie would be the one trial we would have and afterwards we would get years of respite. But Dasah's story shook my understanding of how God worked and pulled back the box I didn't even realize I had put Him in. I did not think this companion of suffering, gripping my hand much more tightly than before, was leading me to God.

It wasn't until I looked back on my prayer for that year (that it would be a year of joy) that I began to see how God would answer that prayer in far different ways than I imagined. Perhaps Dasah had been chosen to be mine for such a time as this to lead not only others, but me to God in a way I had never known.

I looked back on what I had written as the New Year began before we were pregnant with Dasah and before we knew 2014 would unfold so much differently than we had imagined:

> This past year, 2013, has taken a toll on my heart, has left me sweetly broken, and has drawn me to a deeper intimacy with God in the midst of all the questions I now have for Him.
>
> I have experienced His nearness and His love for me in new ways.
>
> And I have found myself with a deeper longing for heaven than I have ever known.
>
> This past year has drawn me into deeper, more authentic relationships with friends, family, and most significantly, my husband. We have fallen in love with each other in ways we never knew possible. The deep joy of welcoming your first child into the world and deep pain of having to bury your first child have forced us to draw near to the Lord and to each other, to learn how to love and how to communicate in ways that have not broken us, but have only served to strengthen our young marriage.
>
> Amid all God has walked us through, all we have gained and lost in 2013 . . . I am convinced it will be the year we look back on as the best year of our lives. It has been a year which has deepened a foundation of faith and trust in our great God that will ripple through generations of the Dennis family to come and will be a marker for us in living out Psalm 145:4 "One generation shall commend your works to another, and shall declare your mighty acts."
>
> Yet, in the still freshness of our grief as a new year begins I find I am so tired. My defenses are down, and my emotions are up. If

you ask me how I'm doing (a genuine, yet often quite overwhelming question for a mother who has just lost her child), I may say "OK" or "fine" or if you're lucky "good." But the true answer would be, "I am deeply sad, missing my little girl always, longing to live out the role of a mother in a very practical way, and simply trusting God (sometimes well, sometimes not) to walk me through each moment of this day . . . and this conversation." So, in my tiredness, sadness, and hope as I look to this year, thinking what do I want to trust the Lord for, my first response has been filled with the desire that this year would bring more joy than sadness, hoping we may welcome another baby into our lives.

And this is where my fear can begin.

For anyone who has walked through tragedy . . . you know. Tragedy can strike at any time, at any place, to anyone. There are no guarantees for us. God held us this last year in profound ways, and you'd think that would translate into a deeper trust in whatever we walk through this year . . . and in some ways it does and in some ways it doesn't. I can't control what this year brings or doesn't bring; I can only trust the One who IS in control and IS good. And this is the war within my heart. Will I fight to control what I can't or trust the One who controls all things?

So what is my hope for 2014? Yes, it is more joy than sorrow. Yes, it is to bring home a baby . . . but even more so, as I've thought about this the past few weeks, my greatest hope for 2014 is not that I would set my gaze on things that are not guarantees but that I would set my gaze on Jesus, finding my greatest hope in Him as I lay my deep longings at His feet and walk in new surrender.

Jesus, He is my only guarantee (and He's a pretty darn good guarantee).

He is the one I'm praying would be the direction of my gaze whatever this year may bring.

I hardly remembered my greatest hope for the year was to fix my gaze on Jesus more fully. Yes, I hoped it would be a year of joy, but the kind of joy that is only able to come from Christ. The kind of joy Tolkien spoke about in his essay on fairy tales, "joy beyond the walls of the world, poignant as grief."[1]

Through much of my journey with Dasah,
the questions and pain I felt was met by
silence from the God who had been so near
to me just a year before.

When I went back and read over what I had written in the early days
of 2014 after finding out Dasah's condition, I wanted to throw that journal
across the room (mad that it wouldn't be the kind of joy I wanted). But as
I sat before God to listen to Him, my defenses began to melt, and my heart
softened as He pointed me to the joy my heart really wanted.

I looked more intently at the verse I had written on the front of my
journal and another I had added later:

> "Weeping may last for the night, But a shout of joy comes
> in the morning." (Psalm 30:5b)

> "If Your presence does not go with us, do not lead us up
> from here." (Exodus 33:15)

I really believed these were the verses God had put on my heart to pray
over and trust Him for the year. But I assumed I knew how He would bring
joy and why we would need His presence to go before us. I began having
opportunities to speak about our story with Sophie; a news channel had
picked up our story and wanted to feature it. It appeared that we had more
and more opportunities to tell the story of what God had done for us with
Sophie. And we realized we needed God to give us wisdom as He led us up
from this place of grief. And then we would have a healthy baby. This was
how He would answer these prayers and bring to life these passages, right?

How many times did I have to remember God's ways are not our ways;
He doesn't do things the way we think He will. As I looked at those verses,
I couldn't for the life of me comprehend how they fit together and how this
could still be a year of unexpected joy. Though I wanted to, in the midst of

my feeble faith, still trust Him for joy this year. No words of comfort or words at all seemed to come from God that day. Only silence.

Through much of my journey with Dasah, the questions and pain I felt were met by silence from the God who had been so near to me just a year before.

🌸🌸🌸

A few weeks later, still wrestling with these verses, God brought to mind another passage. This time I thought He was speaking to me, answering more vaguely than I'd hoped but speaking to my heart nonetheless:

---

Did knowing Jesus cause my heart to burst with such joy that I could still rejoice even in the most sorrowful of seasons? I think I was just beginning to know Jesus like that.

---

"In my presence there is fullness of joy." It seemed to be a piece of a psalm David wrote where he says of God, "You make known to me the path of life; in your presence there is fullness of joy; at your right hand are pleasures forevermore" (16:11 ESV).

When I looked on the surface, all I was experiencing was disappointment. I longed to experience the joy of bringing home a baby, of seeing our family begin to grow and not just saying goodbye to another child, not just burying another dream. But I knew when you peeled back all the layers of my broken heart there was a seed inside that said, "The Joy I really want, the Joy I know I really need, is the kind that comes from being in the presence of God alone."

I didn't know Him like that. I didn't know Him in the ways Paul talks about Jesus when he says, "I count everything as loss because of the surpassing worth of knowing Christ Jesus my Lord" (Philippians 3:8 ESV).

That verse had become a prayer for my life when I was in college. I wanted to know God in the way Paul spoke of, to know what was so marvelous, wonderful, and astounding about Him that I would lose it all just to know Him more. And it was a prayer God was again answering in far different ways than I could have anticipated. I had forgotten how much I had come to know who God was through Sophie's life.

---

It is often in the darkness where God's name
shines the brightest.

---

Did I still want to know God more, even if it came at a great cost?

The answer seemed to be such an easy and obvious yes in seasons where it wasn't costing me much to follow Him. But now, now the answer didn't seem so easy. And yet it seemed my answer mattered now more than ever. I didn't know how to answer that question, but I knew His Word said true joy is found in His presence, and I wanted *that* joy. So, I began to pray that I would discover more fully what it really meant: "In His presence there is fullness of Joy." I realized I could not walk through this year, and I could not experience the kind of joy I longed for, if His presence did not go with us.

❁❁❁

It would be in the midst of deep pain that I would come to know this joy, and perhaps it is the only way to know true joy. For when we know the joy of eternity, the joy of Christ juxtaposed next to our great grief, doesn't it illuminate the redemption, the hope of redemption? It's a joy this side of heaven full of tears; it's a joy Amy Carmichael says that

> is not gush. Joy is not mere jolliness. Joy is perfect
> acquiescence—acceptance, rest—in God's will, whatever
> comes. And that is so only for the soul who delights
> himself in God. Jesus, our Lord, took God as His God

as well as His Father, and that brought Him to say His
delight was "to do the will of Him who sent me" (John
6:38)—even though that meant the cross and such
agony as no man has ever known. To do the will of God
cost Him blood.[2]

This joy comes at a cost. "For the joy set before him he endured the
cross" (Hebrews 12:2 NIV). Joy and sorrow always colliding. Dasah's story
began with a celebration discovering her gender, where every day we had
letters from people encouraging and praying for us. Again, thousands of
people were following the unfolding of her story on my blog, and friends
and family were reaching out to care for us. But no amount of people could
erase the loneliness in my soul as I anticipated the loss of a second child. I
thought as I began to grasp this joy that God was going to write on my soul
that He was leading me to greater heights of hope, but instead it seemed
the way to this hope was through a never-ending wilderness.

And it would be in the wilderness, where hope felt far away and joy
was fleeting, where God was answering that prayer for joy that comes out
of being in God's presence alone. It was a deep kind of joy resounding
and reverberating within the walls of sorrow and suffering. And it was joy
coming in my circumstances (just not the ones I thought it would come
in). I was learning what it meant to, like Paul, experience an abundance of
sorrow and yet still always rejoice (2 Corinthians 6:10). My rejoicing was
not in my circumstances, it was a rejoicing in who God was, and it was a
rejoicing in the midst of tears.

Did knowing Jesus cause my heart to burst with such joy that I could
still rejoice even in the most sorrowful of seasons? I think I was just beginning to know Jesus like that. I prayed I would have the kind of joy John
Piper speaks of: "that would be so salty, so bright. So bright that it would
look like the glory of God on the earth."[3] The kind of joy that would not
be only for me, but for the world to see the One who brings me that kind
of joy. This is the joy God was beginning to give me a taste of, beginning

to write on my heart. The kind of joy that declares, even in the darkest moments: Jesus is my greatest joy. He is my greatest treasure. As Edward Mote said long ago in "My Hope Is Built on Nothing Less":

> His oath. His covenant. His blood.
> Support me in the whelming flood;
> When all around my soul gives way.
> He then is all my hope and stay.

I have most often seen the greatness of our God in the resilience of His people who have suffered deeply and yet still praised Him. When fear surrounded and death was about to envelop His people, He called Esther to be a part of His rescue plan and reveal the greatness and power of His name. It is often in the darkness where God's name shines the brightest.

# SIXTEEN

## The Lonely Places

*Loneliness is a wilderness, but through receiving it as a gift, accepting it from the hand of God, and offering it back to Him with thanksgiving, it may become a pathway to holiness, to glory, and to God Himself.*

—Elisabeth Elliot

O nce again, we sat in the office of our pastor, Renaut, and I wondered if he'd still have a way with his words that would lift us from the pages of our broken story to the pages of eternity. Would he remind us we were still in a story ordained by God—a good story? It was a month before Dasah would make her entrance out of the safe confines of my womb and into the perilous air of this world.

He asked, "How has this journey with Dasah been different than Sophie?"

I looked at Kevin, and tears brimmed at the corners of my eyes. Words began to pour out, slowly, bringing together thoughts that had only begun to form in my heart, into words on my lips.

"It has been more lonely, it has been more difficult, more isolating.

And, yet, while God taught us how to celebrate life in the midst of death with Sophie, Dasah's story has become less about her and more about God. With Dasah, in the midst of the loneliness and sorrow, God has brought more of Himself into focus—that He is worthy of our lives, worthy of our praise no matter the pain, heartache, sorrow, or joy that He asks us to endure."

Renaut probed a little deeper while listening to us speak and said, "While Sophie's story taught you how to celebrate in grief, Dasah's story is teaching you how to suffer in grief. Both lessons hold equally beautiful truths of God that your daughters are teaching you." While people were entering our lives and story, and we continued to celebrate Dasah's life together, it was different. And this time around what we needed was different.

The very nature of grief, sorrow, and suffering is lonely. Often people know how to celebrate and lift your eyes to hope. But it is much more difficult for people to sit in someone's pain and allow it to just be that. Painful. Few people in our culture understand what it looks like to suffer with another. It's quite uncomfortable. Goodness knows it was hard for me to just sit in the pain and not try to find a silver lining or pretty bow to tie everything up with.

Renaut asked us, "What would it look like for people to suffer with you, and for you to press into the loneliness and ask God to meet you there?"

I didn't have an answer to that question. But one thing that continued to come to mind was the reality that often the greatest treasures are discovered in the darkest of places.

I wondered if God was inviting me into the darkness to discover His treasures.

It was almost forty days until Dasah would be born. We had scheduled a C-section for November 13, 2014 (unless she came early). Having walked this road with Sophie, there were many emotions raging in my soul as I looked ahead to the joy of meeting her and the sorrow of knowing that apart from God's miraculous intervention, "goodbyes" would come far too soon. So I thought I'd begin a journey for those forty days of studying people in the Bible who had also been in places of loneliness, isolation, and darkness. I wanted to seek out what treasures of God's character they discovered in their own lonely places. Perhaps their discoveries would become mine.

It's difficult in such a connected society to press into our loneliness. We can easily fill those voids with more Netflix, more absentminded scrolling on social media, more reading of frivolous articles, more exercise, more food, more nights out, instead of pressing into what that loneliness surfaces in our hearts.

Could it be that even loneliness could serve a purpose in our grief? Could it be that even our loneliness held an invitation? I think I was a little afraid to go to those lonely places of my grief.

What would I discover about myself?

About God?

---

I began to grow in learning how to be present in my grief while not ignoring where those closest to me were too.

---

One of the first stories I studied in those forty days was the story of Hagar. It was her story that led me to discover afresh that God sees me in the midst of the deep loneliness of my soul.

⊠⊠⊠

Hagar. Egyptian servant to Abram and Sarai. Used by Sarai to conceive a child through Abram to produce an heir that Sarai thought she could never produce. Sarai didn't trust or perhaps understand that God's promise of an heir would come through her. She was in her late seventies at the time, so it is no wonder she questioned whether God would bless the nations through her womb. She took matters into her own hands, and consequences followed.

Hagar became pregnant and looked with contempt on Sarai for putting herself in this situation (wouldn't you be a little mad?). Sarai, not too happy with Hagar's response, dealt "harshly with her" (Genesis 16:6 ESV), which caused Hagar to flee. And into the wilderness went Hagar.

Alone and pregnant.

---

He sees me, He sees you. He has not forgotten what you are walking through, and He is the One who sees and looks after us—just like He did for Hagar—in the wilderness of our souls.

---

I wonder what she was thinking in her loneliness? Will I survive? How will I carry this child? Is the God of Abram and Sarai my God too?

And there in the wilderness, an angel of the Lord appeared to Hagar, calling her to return to Sarai, to submit to this woman who had just dealt so harshly with her. But He doesn't send her back without a reminder that "the LORD has listened to your affliction" (Genesis 16:11 ESV). And Hagar begins to know this God as intimate with her too. "Then she called the name of the LORD who spoke to her, 'You are a God who sees'; for she said, 'Have I even remained alive here after seeing Him?'" (Genesis 16:13). And it is here where we first see the character of God as the "God who sees—El Roi" show up (Genesis 16:13).

He sees me. This is part of who He is . . . a seeing God.

What does that mean? To see is not just a visual observation but also awareness, a noticing of what it is that your eyes perceive.

My husband has opened my eyes more fully to this word in our marriage. I often become so self-focused, so concerned with my own grief and weariness I fail to see my husband in what he is experiencing and walking through. This was especially true as I carried Dasah, and the weariness in my soul made it difficult to look outside of myself. Kevin would gently tell me at times when I was more inward-focused: "I just don't feel seen by you."

That phrase alone has opened my eyes to what it looks like to be aware through my sight of what my husband is walking through too. Do I see him? So I began to ask him: "Do you feel seen by me?" I began to grow in learning how to be present in my grief while not ignoring where those closest to me were too. I was (and still am) learning what it looks like to truly see others in a knowing, watchful awareness. And yet even though I have failed in my humanness, God does not fail in seeing us.

---

> God won't always rescue us out of the pain and loneliness, but He will rescue us in and through it. This is where He is revealing the treasures of His character that can only be found in the lonely places.

---

At times it "felt" like God was far and that He didn't see. The immense loneliness of my soul caused me to wonder and cry out often, "God, do You see me? Do You see this hurting heart?" Was God really silent to my cries? I wondered if the Lord was seeing in a way that He would do something about what we were walking through.

Hagar's cry, "You are a God of seeing. . . . Truly here I have seen him who looks after me" (Genesis 16:13 ESV), attuned my own eyes to how God was looking after Kevin and me. Was He my seeing God as well? I wanted to know Him that way.

※※※

It was in a seemingly small circumstance just a few days later, where God made me more aware that He sees me and looks after me. Kevin and I were preparing to head to the hospital to go over our birth plan and our desires for what we'd like our time with Dasah to look like. We were delivering at a different hospital for a variety of reasons, one of which was that one of the doctors who specializes in pediatric palliative care (and was a key part of Sophie's birth) no longer lived in town. We wanted to speak with him at some point, and connected with him just twenty minutes before we left for our consultation at the hospital. As Kevin spoke with him about how we should go about this meeting, I couldn't help but think, *God, You see us. You see our needs. You see the details of this journey that can seem overwhelming, the decisions we need to make; You are providing what we need in the most timely of ways.*

I'm not sure I would have been aware of His seeing us in those circumstances had I not just been studying the life of Hagar. But God was attuning my eyes and ears to His seeing ways.

He sees me, He sees you. He has not forgotten what you are walking through, and He is the One who sees and looks after us—just like He did for Hagar—in the wilderness of our souls.

❋❋❋

Though we are created to be in community, there are seasons of our lives when many who love us surround us and care for us—but still an immense loneliness exists in our souls. It exists in the times when you are brutally aware of what you alone are walking through and must walk through. And even when others have walked similar paths, offering you great comfort in the commonality of your journeys, still there is loneliness only you experience. It's found in the person who feels like the outsider in their community, the person who longs for a spouse, the woman and man struggling with infertility, the parent grieved over choices his/her child is making, the person who has just lost a loved one, and the parents carrying a child to term who is not expected to live. And these are only a few of the countless seasons of life that can produce profound loneliness.

As I read Hagar's story, I was struck by the profound sense of loneliness she must have experienced and the fact that it was in those very places of loneliness that God revealed more of Himself to her. We do not see Him revealing Himself to her anywhere else but in the loneliness of her soul, though He may have. But He chose to show us more of His character in these particular moments in Hagar's story. Why?

Though we are created to be in community, we must come to know and understand who our God is in seasons of great loneliness because otherwise we are too inclined to escape the loneliness. We try to fill the void with things that do not fill, to run from the deep recesses of pain and never more fully grasp the sufficiency of Christ in our life. And we are left missing the wonderful reality that in those places of great loneliness, He is enough. And we are most definitely not alone because the God of the universe, Elohim, the Great I Am, is with us.

As Kevin and I were at one of our many doctor appointments, watching Dasah move around on the ultrasound screen, again I couldn't get the story of Hagar out of my mind. Because in her story we see God as not only with her but also with her son. And not only was the God of the universe with Kevin and me, but He was with Dasah. I was reading the passage in Isaiah that Kevin read to me over and over again as I was in labor with Sophie and remembered once again that in the great fears, unknowns, and mountains before us, He goes with us, all of us.

> But now thus says the LORD, he who created you, O Jacob, he who formed you, O Israel: "Fear not, for I have redeemed you; I have called you by name, you are mine. When you pass through the waters, *I will be with you*; and through the rivers, they shall not overwhelm you; when you walk through fire you shall not be burned, and the flame shall not consume you. For I am the LORD your

God, the Holy One of Israel, your Savior." (Isaiah 43:1-3
ESV, emphasis mine)

God won't always rescue us out of the pain and loneliness, but He will rescue us in and through it. This is where He is revealing the treasures of His character that can only be found in the lonely places—treasures that pull us out of the loneliness and into deeper, richer and greater awareness of the profound community we have with our Savior, the One who is walking with us in every season of our lives and giving us His power to experience the richness of community with others. Could I continue to say yes to what He had called me to walk? Could I say like Abraham when God called Him to the most shocking task, "Here I am"?

⊗⊗⊗

"Here I am" (Genesis 22:1). It was the response of Abraham when God called out to him, about to ask Abraham to do the impossible—to sacrifice his only son, the one God himself had promised him and had declared would be a part of God's blessing to the nations. The one who finally came out of Sarai's womb. It was the response that Isaac had to his father, Abraham, as Abraham calls out to find his son to take him on this painful journey. And it was the response of Abraham when he was about to sacrifice his only son and the angel of the Lord calls out from heaven and intervenes. "Here I am."

---

Even in our darkest hour, God's presence
with us cannot help but be displayed through
the life of the one willing to simply depend
on Him.

---

What perplexed me as I read this just a few weeks before Dasah's arrival was that Abraham was not hiding or running from the excruciating task that God had asked of him. Abraham was simply present in his location, ready and willing to respond to his God in whatever He called him into, the known and the unknown. It is a faith you see erupt from a long journey of learning more of the trustworthiness, goodness, and faithfulness of his God.

In what ways did Abraham know his God that he could willingly and without hesitation say, "Here I am"? In what ways did I know my God, the God of Abraham, that enabled me to willingly and without hesitation say, "Here I am"? Would I continue to go where He called me? Would I trust that He would continue to show up along each moment of this journey? And would I willingly and without hesitation say, "Here I am"?

---

And God reveals Himself and His power in
the most unlikely of places so that we and the
watching world around us would know that
He alone is the source of all hope and joy.

---

As the weeks and days grew closer to Dasah's arrival, so did the weight of the pain that was coming. It felt increasingly difficult to say "Here I am," and yet, as I continued to press into the dark places of grief, I discovered in His Word God showing up to man after man, woman after woman in their dark and lonely places. Their strength in their darkness gave me courage.

Dr. Timothy Laniak once said in response to a friend who had suffered devastating loss, "Welcome to the darkness. There are more questions than answers in this place. But you'll find good company among those who understand how little we understand—but still hold on to God's hand."[1]

I indeed had more questions than answers, but I, too, was finding good company in the darkness. And these men and women who had journeyed through their own darkness awakened in my heart God's nearness in the darkness—men like Joseph, whose story God used to reveal in more clarity what it looks like to worship God no matter what.

✿✿✿

Joseph. Favorite son of Jacob, one of twelve sons, sold into slavery by his jealous brothers, enslaved, and then in a strange turn of events appointed the right-hand man to Pharaoh. He is then wrongfully accused by Pharaoh's wife and thrown into prison. Yet, three times we see in Genesis 39 a declaration that the Lord was with Joseph in all of it. The very place where darkness should surround, the Lord showed Joseph his steadfast love and gave him favor—even in prison. "And whatever [Joseph] did, the LORD made to prosper" (Genesis 39:23).

My first thought was if God's presence with Joseph made him succeed and prosper everywhere he went, then how did Joseph end up in prison? Oh the ways of God are not like my ways. My idea of prospering was not like His, and in this very broken world over and over, God was revealing that even in the brokenness, even in the darkness, even in the places where it didn't make any sense how we got there, He was present. His presence was more than enough to sustain and carry me.

There was one statement in this passage that gave me a profound glimpse into Joseph's heart and perspective. When trying to be persuaded by his master's wife to lie (have sex) with her he responded, "How then could I do this great evil and sin against God?" (Genesis 39:9). I noticed a piece of Joseph's heart to honor and fear God in whatever circumstances, as challenging as they may be. Even in our darkest hour, God's presence with us cannot help but be displayed through the life of the one willing to simply depend on Him.

A woman named Nancy, who has also walked a road filled with loss, reminded me of the true miracle of what God produces in our lives when we trust Him. We were talking of my hope for God to heal Dasah, and she said, "Do not forget that the miracle will also be to have joy in the midst of sorrow, peace when there should be no peace, hope when all seems hopeless. When joy and hope and peace are found in seasons of such loss, that, too, is a miracle that could only be wrought by the supernatural work of the Holy Spirit in the life of a believer."

Only God, through His Spirit, who lives in the life of every person who knows Jesus, can and will produce such fruit in seasons of such darkness. I wondered if this was how I would see and how others would see the greatness of God. To know Him on the mountaintop is one thing, but to know and still praise Him in the valley of the shadow of death, well that is quite another. John Piper once said:

> I think the tang of the salt that the world needs to taste, and the brightness of the light that the world needs to see is precisely this indomitable joy in the midst of sorrow. Joy in the midst of health? Joy in the midst of wealth and ease? And when everyone speaks well of you? Why would that mean anything to the world? They have that already. But indomitable joy in the midst of sorrow—that they don't have. That is what Jesus came to give in this fallen, pain-filled, sin-wrecked world.[2]

It was only the supernatural work of God and His presence with Joseph that could make him prosper during slavery and imprisonment, revealing a picture of God's steadfast love and favor in the midst of betrayal. Joseph displayed a fear of God in the midst of the most challenging of circumstances. And it was only the supernatural work of God, through His Spirit, that could enable Kevin and me to prosper and know God's love and favor toward us in the midst of the darkness we were in. The same God who was with Hagar in the desert, Abraham on the mountaintop, and Joseph in prison was with Kevin and me. And God reveals Himself and His power in the most unlikely of places so that we and the watching world around us would know that He alone is the source of all hope and joy.

# SEVENTEEN

## WORSHIPPING IN THE DARKNESS

*Paul did not carry a cemetery with him, but a chorus of victorious praise; and the harder the trial, the more he trusted and rejoiced, shouting from the very altar of sacrifice.*

—Lettie Cowman

Sometimes I imagined what life would be like if this season of darkness and loss and loneliness were just a terrible dream and never really happened. What would life be like if I was chasing after a one-year-old who was learning to walk and mumble sounds that had the resemblance of words and then stress about how I was going to handle a newborn. I became the most discontent and unsatisfied when I thought of what my life could've been. It's an unhealthy place to be, but let's be honest, it's a place all of us are tempted to linger in for a little too long when we are in the midst of the hardness of life.

The grass is always greener somewhere else . . . right?

I was learning that it's OK to want out of these situations, but also what it looks like to choose to be in the place of darkness that God has called me to and walk with Him there. Joseph lived like this. He lived like

God was so worthy that he would be faithful to Him even when every circumstance seemed to contradict God's faithfulness.

---

It had been in the places I thought I was least
likely to find treasures where I had
only begun to discover a God who
delivers us to *Him*.

---

The more I read Joseph's story, the more I was amazed at the man. He wanted out, too, and yet it's what he did with that desire to get out that gripped my heart.

Joseph was in prison and had just interpreted a man's dream (who will soon be released) when Joseph said to him: "Only remember me, when it is well with you, and please do me the kindness to mention me to Pharaoh, and so get me out of this house. For I was indeed stolen out of the land of the Hebrews, and here also I have done nothing that they should put me into the pit" (Genesis 40:14-15 ESV).

So what happens?

"Yet the chief cupbearer did not remember Joseph, but forgot him" (Genesis 40:23 ESV). And for two more years, Joseph was left in prison.

At this point Joseph had been in Egypt for at least eleven years, and though I don't know how long he had been in prison, it is clear that things weren't necessarily getting better for him. Wouldn't you want out? Wouldn't you say, "Get me out of this house—this prison! I was wrongfully put here; I did nothing to deserve this. Please tell who needs to be told that I don't belong here."

In our own culture of comfort and ease, we can often either grow bitter toward this God we serve when things don't go our way, or we do everything we can to get out of the circumstance in which we find ourselves.

Yet, this is not what Joseph did. He was honest about wanting out and yet was faithful in the darkness.

Joseph continued to honor God; he attributed God's power where God's power was due. Somewhere along the way God built in Joseph a deep understanding of Himself that continued to sustain and dictate how Joseph lived—so much so that seven years after Joseph was released from prison, and from the highest position of authority next to Pharaoh, he was able to say, "For God has made me fruitful in the land of my affliction" (Genesis 41:52 ESV).

❀❀❀

Life hadn't gone the way I had hoped, and I was discovering that these afflictions were, in fact, a part of the good chapters in our lives. Even the days before Dasah was born and would most likely die, I thought of all the goodness in these chapters already. I thought of all the joy, life, and hope! It is often hard to see the joy, life, and hope in the midst of painful circumstances, deep disappointment, and sorrow.

> I could not begin to understand all the ways
> His sovereignty worked or played out in my
> life, but I knew I served a good God—a God
> who was loving, kind, and for us.

But these were the chapters that were leading me to more of Jesus than I could ever know I could experience, to more hope planted in the right places than I even knew needed to be dug up and replanted. And these were the chapters leading me to a joy more firmly rooted in Christ than I knew He could give. I prayed that I could say the same words as Joseph, "God has made me fruitful in the land of my affliction." In it—not out of it. That is who my God was, and who He continued to be to Kevin and me—my God who was meeting us *in* our affliction.

It had been in the places I thought I was least likely to find treasures where I had only begun to discover a God who delivers us to *Him*.

God had sent us to this place of darkness; I could not begin to make sense of it. But as I dug further in His Word, I continued to learn how to bring my pain to Him. And He met me in the pain.

Joseph had this perspective, as He was able to see a fuller glimpse of all the tragedy He had experienced, the losses and pain, only to discover that He was a part of a greater plan to preserve His people. It's crazy, when he meets his brothers again who had sold him into slavery and says: "For God *sent* me before you to preserve life. . . . For God *sent* me before you to preserve for you a remnant. . . . So it was not you who *sent* me here, but God" (Genesis 45:5-8 ESV, emphasis mine).

---

How amazing would it be if this generation of believers walked through seasons of darkness and reflected and showed the world that Jesus is our great treasure, that He's worth knowing, worth following, and worthy of our worship in any circumstance and any season?

---

Would God ever allow and, yes, even send us to a place of darkness if only for us to find that it is the very place where He would bring life and light not only to us but also to the world around us?

One prayer I had since finding out Dasah's diagnosis was that both she and Sophie would be givers of life. I prayed that their lives would give life to other children in unexpected ways.

I prayed that we, their parents, in walking this journey would steward well the gift of their lives to us. I prayed we would step into the platforms we never wanted but now had to speak on grief, loss, surrender, the sanctity of life, and be ourselves life-givers to others in the midst of our own sadness.

And I have prayed that our little girls would lead others to the One true God, the true life giver, Jesus Christ, who is the way, the truth, and the life (John 14:6). To live this way is a daily surrender to the very One who sent me to this place, to let Him refine, restore, and meet me in the darkness.

He had not sent Kevin and me to this place in vain, because of some random genetic glitch (or whatever else has caused the lives of our children to unfold in the way that it has, about which our doctors still have no clear answer). God is in our story, and even as I write that with tears in my eyes, I am asking God to help me remember that on the days where the sorrow is too great, and I watch others walk a seemingly easier road, wondering what He's sent us here for, that I play a small part in a bigger story God is writing for all creation.

I could not begin to understand all the ways His sovereignty worked or played out in my life, but I knew I served a good God—a God who was loving, kind, and for us. A God who continued to demonstrate these aspects of His character to generations past and generations future. He was involved in my life. He would redeem these broken pieces. And He sends those who have a relationship with Him into a broken world to take their own broken pieces and be vehicles of bringing His light, His life into the watching world.

Joseph was not the only one sent to preserve life. So are we as Christ-followers. Sent to be the salt of the earth (Matthew 5:13). Sent to be the light of the world (v. 14). Sent to be witnesses of His power and grace to the ends of the earth (Acts 1:8). Sent to be ministers of reconciliation and ambassadors for Christ (2 Corinthians 5:18). Sent to show the watching world that Jesus is our greatest treasure.

This story He was writing for us was not the way I would choose to show the watching world that He is my treasure. I'm sure that there were many times when Joseph would not have chosen the story written for him to be a vehicle to saving God's people. "God, isn't there another way?" is what my heart cried often. And Jesus cried out the same when He was about to go to the cross to take on the sins of the world. "My Father, if it be possible, let this cup pass from me; nevertheless, not as I will, but as you will" (Matthew 26:39 ESV).

I was not alone in this cry; Jesus Himself walked a similar road. Countless faithful men and women have honored God in wherever He sent them and so have been lights of His power and grace to the world. I prayed that I would be a part of a generation that reflected what generations past have—that we would live as sent ones. That we would walk with God in the midst of the unknown and the dark places where we wonder what purpose they could possibly play in the grand story. How amazing would it be if this generation of believers walked through seasons of darkness and reflected and showed the world that Jesus is our great treasure, that He's worth knowing, worth following, and worthy of our worship in any circumstance and any season?

And so, the week before Dasah's birth (as God was writing all of these truths on my heart as only He could do), Kevin and I decided to honor Dasah's life, to reflect what God had been doing in our own hearts, and that the only proper way to spend our potentially last evening with her was to invite our community of family and friends to worship with us.

God had so moved in our hearts that our prayers began to be less and less "God, heal our daughter" but "God be glorified." I still longed for healing. I still thought surely God would heal this time (because that's the only way I could make sense of God asking us to walk this journey twice). But the desire for healing that week before her arrival was second to my desire to see God's name and glory lifted high, in our home, in our life, and in that hospital.

❖❖❖

Our family arrived earlier in the week and gathered in our home that had become this sacred place of worship. This time they were all wearing matching pink-and-white "Supporting C.A.S.T." T-shirts. They handed me one that said "Mommy" with a silver star on my belly (with Dasah's name in the star), and Kevin was given a shirt that said "Daddy."

I was overwhelmed with their presence and commitment to walk this journey with us, again. Friends trickled in, and my nephews were running around, occasionally coming over to touch my belly and say hi to Dasah. The smiles and the tears ran freely.

---

> I trusted God's ways above our own,
> convinced in those moments that hoping
> in Him was better than hoping in things
> of this world.

---

It was strange to know the next morning I would hold and meet my second daughter. What would she look like? Would she be born alive? Would we be able to bring her home? Would God heal her? All my heart could do that day before was look up, to rest my questions in the arms of my Savior, and trust Him for what would unfold. Peace reigned over my heart that day. Supernatural peace. Miraculous peace.

I can only attribute such peace to the hundreds and even thousands of people praying for us and for His Spirit to continually work in our lives.

His grace was covering us in ways I had not known could happen.

That evening, our friends gathered throughout our house to worship. And my family huddled together in the hope room.

❈❈❈

The Hope Room. It's what we call it. It's the odd room many homes have where you put a formal living area that no one ever sits in. So when we first knew we'd be moving to this home, I wanted to make it the kids' playroom. Full of hope for this second child I was carrying, not knowing her condition at the time, I wanted that room to be for that child (and the many more I assumed would come) to play in and destroy.

---

There is something about discovering the Lord in the deep places of grief, loneliness, and heartache that drives your heart to a greater sense of His worthiness of our praise and worship.

---

I love designing, and I dreamed of the cute furniture I'd put there, the decorations, the place for toys and artwork. And then we found out Dasah's condition, and I stood at the edge of this little front room with tears in my eyes, wondering, "Now what do I do?"

*Make it a room of hope*, a small, soft thought came in my mind. Hope not just for more kids but also as a declaration that Kevin and I trust how God will fill our home and lives with children. And so the Hope Room was created, and friends and family partnered with us and filled the room with treasures and beauty that reflected our story and our hope. We turned the far wall into a giant chalkboard wall, and that week Kevin's dad, Jim, and best friend, Craig, installed white crown molding around the black chalk paint to make it really pop.

With the help of my mother-in-law, we painted twenty frames a vintage white color, slightly distressed, and filled them with photos from left to right on the wall above a long olive-green couch. The photos told our story, with a giant photo in the middle of the bright balloons we released the day we buried Sophie.

I had written in white script on the chalkboard across the entire top: "The Best Is Yet to Come." My mom helped me repaint an ugly brown coffee table olive green to use as an art table. Friends bought a teal and white zigzag carpet to cover the floor. I used the colorful backdrop of tied fabric strings I had made for Sophie's one year of life celebration as the "curtains" to frame the window with color. My sister-in-law, Mayra, sent kids' books, a wall bookshelf, and countless costumes. Over time, my dad added handmade wooden blocks, much like the ones I grew up with. And my brother Dan sent a beautiful piece of artwork using pins and strings stuck in a piece of wood to create an anchor—a reminder that God is the anchor of our hope.

The Hope Room was finished the day before Dasah was born. My nephews played in that room, pulling out the superhero costumes and creating artwork we would hang on the wall. I smiled through tears thinking of how children, who may not be our own, would delight in this space. And I trusted God's ways above our own, convinced in those moments that hoping in Him was better than hoping in things of this world.

I sat in the Hope Room the morning before Dasah's birth, reading from Isaiah 25 and looking at the sweet footprint of Sophie sitting atop those profound verses—which held the promise of our tears being wiped away and death being no more. I thought of when Dasah's footprint would sit next to her big sister's, and how they would meet and know each other long before I would get the opportunity.

❈❈❈

The night before Dasah's birth, we sat in that room and worshipped and prayed for God to be glorified and His peace to reign in our hearts and our minds. It was holy ground.

My friends Brandon, Mac, Jen, Elyse, and Jennafer stood in the dining room, dining table moved aside, guitars in the guys' hands and angelic voices on the girls' lips, lifting our eyes to God as we sang songs that held great meaning to us on this journey. The songs were interspersed with times of prayer. It was like a sweet aroma of praise was being lifted to heaven as I sat on the floor next to Kevin—in between the Hope Room and the living room, in front of the angelic voices. A sweet photo was taken as my family prayed over Dasah, my five-year-old nephew with his hand on my belly.

The tears flowed that evening, but joy ruled my heart—joy that our little daughter had so lifted our eyes to who our God is. Worthy, worthy, worthy to be praised.

If there was anything I had learned in the weeks leading up to this day as I purposely engaged with God in the lonely places of my grief—journeying with men and women of the Bible to the places of darkness where they found themselves in desperation before their God—it was that their affliction drew their hearts to worship. There is something about discovering the Lord in the deep places of grief, loneliness, and heartache that drives your heart to a greater sense of His worthiness of our praise and worship.

I could think of no better way to spend the last night we may have with our little girl than in praise to the One she may soon meet. Oh, how we prayed she would meet Him face-to-face much, much later in life. But whether God would heal our little girl the following day—this side of heaven or the other—I knew we would still worship His holy name. For He is worthy of worship simply because of Who He is. And I would embrace the joy and pain that would follow, even when it hurt so badly I could hardly breathe.

# EIGHTEEN

## Eight Twenty-Five

*But if we hope for what we do not see,*
*we wait for it with patience.*

—The apostle Paul

It was November 13, 2014, early in the morning. Kevin and I walked into the hospital with nervous excitement, anticipation, hope, and sadness, as we knew the day had come to meet our second daughter face-to-face. To love her face-to-face. To know her face-to-face. And to perhaps say good-bye to her face-to-face. I had hoped and prayed that the miracle God would choose would be one of a miraculous healing of Dasah's brain and skull. Or at the very least, He would sustain her life for a few days and we could bring her home with us. I had hoped for more time. But truth be told, anything less than a lifetime with her would not have been enough. I hoped for many things I would not see that day, and still many more that in time I would see.

Two nurses, Sarah and Lauren, greeted us warmly at 5:30 a.m. in the lobby outside of the entrance to the labor and delivery floor. My anxiety for the day ahead slowly melted as they hugged me, tears in their own eyes, and I knew we were in good hands.

While they prepared me for surgery, Sarah asked if I'd want to listen to Dasah's heartbeat one last time. The perfect rhythmic sounds of her little heart carried such beauty. And the tears flowed as I hoped that this would not be the last time we would hear her sweet heartbeat. Our family and pastor, Renaut, soon came in to pray over the three of us and speak words of truth and hope, knowing our fears may cloud those truths, knowing we needed others to surround us in the heaviness and uncertainties of these moments leading up to Dasah's arrival. The eyes of my parents and siblings radiated their love for Dasah as they placed their hands over my belly, bowed their heads, and prayed for what would unfold that day.

As we gathered together to pray in our little hospital room, our friends gathered to pray in a waiting area outside the halls where we would deliver Dasah. They began in the wee hours of the morning and continued until the evening, filling the walls of that hospital with praise as they worshipped God together. Stations of prayer were set up in that waiting area, and blankets that our friends Elyse, Jennafer, and many others had prayed over were being set out for our family who would spend the day in a more private waiting area above the one where our friends were gathering. Flowers and treats were scattered throughout the room for our family by the little army gathered in the atrium below, eagerly awaiting what God would do with Dasah's life. My friend, Katie, who prays with power and persistence, said, "We were praising His name on your behalf!"

When our family left, they were ushered to see the team of people that had gathered just below them to pray for Dasah . . . their niece, granddaughter, and cousin about to be born. Their sweet songs of praise filled that atrium and entered the family waiting area, giving courage and strength to our family—who also felt the great weight and heaviness of what was about to unfold. It was like a little army had gathered outside our hospital doors to fight for Dasah and us.

Kevin and I spent a quiet moment, just the three of us, praying and worshipping to Chris Tomlin's song "Whom Shall I Fear—God of Angel

Armies." And we surrendered over and over again our lives, our daughter to our God, who commanded the angels, who went before us.

I was so nervous, so full of fear, hope, and anxiety running all together as the time had come to meet Dasah. The nurses soon came to wheel me into the operating room, leaving Kevin waiting until he would be allowed in, and me trying to be brave and hold back the fearful tears in my eyes.

❖❖❖

Once again I was in another icy-cold operating room, surrounded by a sea of nurses and doctors who would be there to take care of Dasah and me. The room was much bigger than the one I had been in with Sophie and felt much more terrifying. Perhaps because I had been there before, and I knew what was coming.

---

Whereas meeting Sophie had been a pure explosion of love and joy, meeting Dasah was an explosion of love so quickly dampened by the extreme sadness that I now knew with certainty we would have to say goodbye to her soon. We would have to bury a second child.

---

An eerie silence hovered under the bright lights and dull sound of the machines as everyone in the room seemed to feel the weight of this moment. You could cut the tension in the air with a knife. Which is no pun intended since I was about to go under the knife.

My OB, Dr. K, held my hand on the table, speaking courage into my fearful heart as we waited for my high-risk doctor, Dr. A, to come in. He's the one whose seriousness and professionalism we had broken through to discover a tender and loving man who deeply cared for our child and us. He came over with red socks in his hand for my cold feet. I laughed, feigning offense when I saw them and said, "Why didn't you bring pink?" He smiled and laughed with me, as did the rest of the room. The tension had been cut—not with a knife but with laughter.

Laughter even in the anticipation of death.

And then they all went to work. Dr. K. held me tight while I waited for the epidural. I still don't know and don't want to know how long the needle was that was inserted in my lower back as I sat on the edge of the table. A quick jolt of what I can only describe as electricity shot down my legs as my lower body went numb. Within seconds they moved my legs up on the table, laid me down, and did the necessary checks to make sure the anesthesia had worked.

I quickly felt like I was hyperventilating: from the cold, from the fear, from the anxiety, from not having Kevin by my side yet. My brain a bit fuzzy, I needed him there. I began to shake uncontrollably. Where was he? They put oxygen on me fairly quickly, and finally he was there. I calmed down with his presence.

He looked me intently in the eyes and gripped my hand with tenderness and firmness. "I'm here, I'm here. Jesus is here, Jesus is here." And he began to pray with power, conviction, and urgency.

While Kevin prayed, I faintly heard the song "It Is Well" playing softly in the background. I soon felt the pressure, the pressure I knew and remembered from Sophie's birth. The pressure that says, "She's coming." She's coming! Would she be healed? This time I thought she must.

The blue curtain at my shoulders blocked my view. And then she was there and the curtain was pulled down and Dr. K. lifted her high. Her arms stretched wide just like her sister's.

"Free!"

Free from the womb, I immediately knew she would be freed from this life soon too.

Whereas meeting Sophie had been a pure explosion of love and joy, meeting Dasah was an explosion of love so quickly dampened by the extreme sadness that I now knew with certainty we would have to say goodbye to her soon. We would have to bury a second child.

As they took her to clean her off and suction her, I turned my head to Kevin with tears in my eyes. "He didn't heal her. He didn't heal her," were the first whispered words on my lips. I wish those had not been my first words, but they were. And God was in those moments of disappointment, of confusion, still ever-tenderly turning my heart to Him. His unwavering faithfulness to me would hold me in the midst of my wavering moments of faith.

Nancy, one of Dasah's nurses, quickly brought her to me. She was wrapped in the pink knitted blanket I had joyfully spent far too many late nights making so that the first warmth on her skin would be made by me. And all disappointment melted away as I looked with love and joy at those chubby cheeks, sweet lips, and nose that were all Kevin.

She was alive.

My sadness was quickly tempered with overwhelming gratefulness that God had given her breath.

For how long?

I did not know as we held her and loved her.

Kevin quickly began to talk and talk and talk to her, and pretty soon the most precious sounds began to rise from her sweet lips. It seemed as though she was talking back, with the sweetest coos I had ever heard.

I had wondered if I could love a second child as much as I loved Sophie—and as any parent will tell you, your heart for your children just keeps expanding. I loved her every bit as much as her big sister.

I knew my family was packed into the viewing area. My nurse, Sarah, came over with a huge smile earlier to tell me right before surgery that when she went back to get the family to come to the viewing room, she was surprised that everyone in that waiting room followed her to a room meant for only four, maybe five. At least ten crammed in, looking, watching, and waiting.

I knew even with all of the drugs flowing through my body that they were so eager to see Dasah up close.

---

God graciously gave us sweet memories in the midst of the ones we still did not see realized.

---

"Take her over to the window," I said to Kevin with joy on my face.

How I wanted to share this joy of a little girl with the world. I wanted her to experience love from as many people as possible. And I wanted my family and close friends, who loved her so deeply, to have every opportunity they could to pour that love onto her.

Of course I wanted her all to myself. But love gives, love doesn't hold on. Love opens the door for others to experience the same love you are getting to experience even if it costs you much.

Kevin brought her back after everyone gushed with joy after seeing her through the window. I tried to get a good look at her lying down as I wrapped my fingers around her tiny ones and simply delighted in her coos. Dr. K said, "She's quite the talker," while she stitched me up.

"Is that normal?" I wondered, asking Nancy, who was keeping a vigilant eye on Dasah for any signs of distress. With laughter in her voice, she said, "She just has a lot to say." Kevin couldn't stop talking back to her, and they had quite the conversation in that room as I memorized every detail of my little girl's face. And delight washed over me as Dasah's tiny fingers reached out to me and grasped my nose.

They finally put her on my chest, and I exploded in laughter when she proceeded to lift up her face, purse her lips, and as if to pose for Amanda, our photographer, tilted her head right toward the camera. My little ham. My little extrovert. She was just like her daddy in every way.

❉❉❉

We had little expectation for the time we would get to spend with Sophie, not knowing if it would be minutes or hours, and we just hoped to get to hear the sound of her cries. But our time with Dasah was filled with expectation because of the time we *did* get with Sophie. I now was brutally aware of all of the things I wished I could have done with Sophie that I was never able to do. And I wanted to cram as many of those moments in the day with Dasah. It made the day riddled with much more anxiety. I wish I could have laid those expectations down, but I wanted to figure out how to create a lifetime of memories in just a few short hours.

Unrealistic. Yes.

Impossible. Of course.

I still tried.

---

> It seemed this is what our lives had truly become—a constant, daily, moment-by-moment surrender to His plan above our own.

---

And in my angst, God graciously gave us sweet memories in the midst of the ones we did not see realized. I watched Kevin give her a bath as she wiggled and squirmed like any newborn would, her naked body longing for the warmth of her blanket. Kevin and I both enjoyed skin-to-skin time with her, watching her coo and cuddle quietly, our hearts beating together as one.

Together we dressed her in a beautiful pink lace outfit, one we hoped would be her coming-home outfit. Kevin swaddled her to perfection in the blankie her Nini made for her, one just like her big sister's. And I experienced the newness of attempting to breastfeed as she rooted and looked for where to get her food. It was something Sophie never did and that I only dreamed of experiencing with Dasah. It was one of the sweetest gifts of the day, to experience, but for a brief moment, the bond that comes from breastfeeding your child.

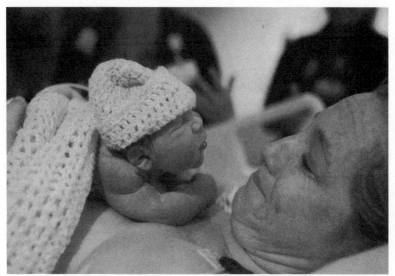

Amanda Kern, Now I Lay Me Down to Sleep Volunteer Photographer

Kevin changed her diaper earlier in the day, and as I gained energy and was able to sit up, I, too, experienced that task—another memory I had not been able to have with Sophie. Another moment of feeling as though I was able to experience some parenting rites of passage. Who knew the joy that could come from the simplicity of changing a diaper?

We watched joy erupt on the faces of our parents when they walked in to meet their newest granddaughter without a wall of glass between them. Their grins were so wide, their pride so deep, their love so strong for this little girl.

Dasah decided to put on a little show and blow bubbles when my siblings and best friends came in. Laughter and joy erupted at the delight of getting a glimpse at Dasah's personality.

As our small group of family and friends gathered to celebrate Dasah's life in our small hospital room, word spread fast throughout the hospital of the arrival of this little girl and of the army of friends and family that had gathered to love her for the short life she would be given.

Chaplains made comments of how in all their years at the hospital they had never seen anything like what they saw that day. In some areas of the hospital, staff were bringing other staff in small groups to just go and watch this little community that was still worshipping, praying, and lifting up their hearts to Jesus on behalf of Dasah's little life.

---

This was part of our journey, part of the reality of walking through a story such as ours, part of loving Dasah, embracing the joy and the sorrow, and loving her in it. She was worth every tear of sorrow and joy that fell that day and every tear that has fallen since.

---

Once again, friends brought a beautiful cake, this time with flowers covering it to celebrate Dasah's birthday. It came from the same restaurant that had made Sophie's cake. Once they heard our story and that there were so many people gathered to celebrate Dasah's life, they gifted not only the cake with flowers but also another cake for the entourage of people. They also catered lunch for my family that day. All free of charge.

Everyone gathered around Dasah and me to sing happy birthday to her. Kevin sang with gusto, me softly, struggling to experience the joy in those moments, knowing so much sadness was coming. Kevin, always knowing how to insert joy into sadness, dipped his finger in the cake and put a little on Dasah's nose, much to my dismay, and laughter arose. Laugher and sorrow, joy and pain, colliding in these sacred moments.

Renaut was there to lead us in a baby dedication as we, for the first time with Dasah outside of the womb, dedicated her to Jesus in front of family and friends. We again submitted our lives and her life to whatever story God would unfold for her. It seemed this is what our lives had truly become—a constant, daily, moment-by-moment surrender to His plan above our own. And Dasah talked the whole way through, her little hand peeking out of her swaddle as if giving a wave to everyone.

I joyfully watched as her grandparents, aunts and uncles, and friends all held her with such love and tenderness. I delighted in seeing my three nephews proudly holding her on the ugly green vinyl couch. Isaac, the oldest, held her, and he did so with seriousness, caution, and such care for her as Jordan, the second-oldest, held his little brother, Jude, not so tenderly.

Around noon, the joy began to turn more somber when our nurses began to notice that Dasah was never quite getting enough oxygen. So as we decided to give her oxygen, the painful realization that we might not get to bring her home with us began to break me. Another prayer God would answer no to. Another crushing disappointment. Again, we would have to say goodbye to our child in the hospital. Again, I would be wheeled out of a hospital bearing all the marks of birth, but with no baby in my arms. Again, I would walk through the door of our home and all the tears shed would be by Kevin and me, not by our little baby crying.

I had prayed that even if God chose not to heal her, He would allow us to bring her home. I couldn't handle so many noes in that moment, but somehow I knew God could handle my bitter disappointment. And so we embraced the tears and the joy that came throughout that day.

---

In that moment, so consumed with grief, I didn't realize that even in the timing of Dasah's life and death, God was pointing us to hope—hope that is beyond the grave, hope that can be seen and known in the darkest places, and hope that is not dependent on our circumstances or our feelings.

---

This was part of our journey, part of the reality of walking through a story such as ours, part of loving Dasah, embracing the joy and the sorrow, and loving her in it. She was worth every tear of sorrow and joy that fell that day and every tear that has fallen since.

Before our family and friends left to give us some time alone, they all laid hands on Dasah, again entrusting her to the Lord and lifting our eyes to the One, the only One, who was giving her breath.

As we enjoyed sweet time with Dasah, we also wanted more people to get to meet her and love on her! So we invited our little army that had been praying for her all day up to meet her. I loved getting to see so many of our friends delight in her, hear her voice, and meet her face-to-face! I let everyone (who had washed their hands) touch her oh-so-soft cheeks. I took great joy in asking our friends, "Do you want to touch her cheek?" and seeing how excited they were just to get to touch Dasah!

Our photographers, Scott and Amanda, who had also photographed and videoed Sophie's life, took beautiful photographs and video of Dasah and us as a family, documenting much of the day. And our friend Elyse stayed to photograph the rest. They were like family to us, stepping into some of the most sacred moments of our lives and beautifully capturing these moments that we would never forget.

The time came where all became quiet in our room, and only Elyse huddled almost invisible to us in the corner—capturing every waking moment with Dasah. Kevin and I read the letters we had each written for her and prayed over her, just the two of us. And as we finished, we looked up to see Elyse's tear-stained face and knew how emotional it was for her to just watch us; she loved Dasah so much too. We told her to put the camera down and come join us as we read to Dasah from the same book we read to Sophie, *On the Night You Were Born*.

Nurses helped us take Dasah's footprints, and I put one of those footprints in my Bible next to Sophie's, on that significant verse in Isaiah—the one where it says that God will one day swallow up death and wipe away tears, and we will declare that we have waited for Him! That's our hope, in Jesus, in the hope He brings because He came and the hope He gives because He's coming back. We're waiting for Him to redeem it all! And oh, how I groaned with longing for that day.

> What I didn't think about until much later
> was how much of a privilege it was to groan,
> how much of a privilege it was to taste this
> groan, for how could I eagerly await redemp-
> tion if I was not brutally aware of my need
> for it and of this world's need for it.

Before Dasah was born, there was a photo taken of everyone praying for her, hands on my bulging belly, and I noticed in the picture that my mom had opened her Bible and put her hand on a passage of Scripture. I later asked her what passage she had laid her hand on. She said, "Psalm 34, which says, 'Those who look to Him are radiant, and their faces shall never be ashamed'" (34:5 ESV). One thing I had been praying for was that our faces would be radiant as we looked to Him at Dasah's birth. There were so many radiant faces of our family and others as we all met her. When I tell others about her even now, I smile and I pray the Lord radiates His joy! She made us all smile.

As I remember this day, looking at the photos, remembering the

Amanda Kern, Now I Lay Me Down to Sleep Volunteer Photographer

moments of joy and sorrow, I feel that Dasah's life (in every way) radiated the Lord's joy into our lives and the lives around us.

🙨🙨🙨

It was 8:25 a.m. when our sweet little girl was born, and it was 8:25 p.m. when she went to be with Jesus.

Her death was not peaceful; it was sudden, quick, and traumatic for me. Nurses remarked that they had never seen anyone go so fast. One of them had looked up and marked the time: 8:25 p.m. Exactly twelve hours.

In that moment, so consumed with grief, I didn't realize that even in the timing of Dasah's life and death, God was pointing us to hope—hope that is beyond the grave, hope that can be seen and known in the darkest places, and hope that is not dependent on our circumstances or our feelings.

Dasah's journey had been consistently about hope for me and for Kevin. Where will we put our hope? What is the hope that doesn't disappoint? Romans 8 had been significant to us, but we did not realize that Romans 8:25 speaks specifically to hope: "But if we hope for what we do not see, we wait for it with patience" (ESV).

I hoped for many things as Dasah passed away. I hoped for more time with her. I hoped for God to heal our sad hearts, I hoped for God to still fill our home with the chaos of children, and most of all I hoped for the day when Jesus will come back and make all things new and I will get to be with Him and our two little girls.

The things I hoped for did not come to be that day, and I felt with poignancy the groan that Paul speaks of earlier in Romans when he says, "For we know that the whole creation groans and suffers the pains of childbirth together until now. . . . We ourselves groan within ourselves, waiting eagerly for our adoption as sons, the redemption of our body" (Romans 8:22). That day in the midst of the joy of knowing and loving Dasah, we could see and feel with glaring certainty that all had not been redeemed.

What I didn't think about until much later was how much of a privilege it was to groan, how much of a privilege it was to taste this groan, for how could I eagerly await redemption if I was not brutally aware of my need for it and of this world's need for it. Yes, hope was a theme for our story with Dasah, but we would not, could not, know this hope apart from knowing the groan. This hope points to the reality that I'm hoping for it because it has not happened yet. Have you thought about the fact that one day hope may no longer exist because we will have and know with full assurance, confidence, and clarity all the promises and the redemption that we have been waiting to know in their fullness?

That day of seeing and knowing felt so far away.

I took such joy in the time that I was able to spend with my sweet little girl, and I groaned when I said goodbye to her lifeless body and felt the deep chasm between life and death, between the here and the not yet. And after nine months and twelve hours with her, the loss of my second daughter plunged me into a place of deeper groaning and grief than I had ever known. It also brought me face-to-face with my Savior, allowing the groan to point me to the Hope for which we wait.

# NINETEEN

## The Lamenting Heart

*He gives me beauty for ashes, the oil of joy for mourning and the garment of praise for the spirit of heaviness. But He doesn't just drop it in my lap, I have to give him the ashes. I have to give Him my mourning, I have to surrender the spirit of heaviness and the exchange takes place. When I come to the cross, I have to give him my sins and what does He give me, His righteousness. I give Him my losses. He gives me gain. I give Him my sorrows. He gives me joy. This is the exchanged life, the crucified life.*

—Elisabeth Elliot

When Dasah passed away, part of me once again died. Just like Sophie, we gathered together in that little hospital room and sang the lyrics to "How Great Is Our God." This time I sang those words with less conviction and more agony filling my heart, hoping against hope that God would reveal Himself once again as He had over the past several years.

How much darkness can the soul contain?

Perhaps a better question would have been how much light could the soul discover in the darkness?

204

A few weeks later, we were driving through those old iron gates of the little cemetery where we had buried our first daughter fourteen months before. How could we be doing this again?

The same people were there, with a few new friends who had entered the sorrow of this season, the weight of it all so much heavier. We still managed smiles as we filled her much prettier casket (we had learned from the first time) with flower stickers covered in notes, and Kevin and I placed our blue and pink respective handprints on the casket. When we buried Sophie, an unexpected joy had infused the day, but a heavy mist clouded that joy when we buried her little sister.

I could hardly comprehend that I was sitting at the burial of my second daughter, the headstone of her sister next to Dasah's casket. It reads:

Sophia Kyla Dennis

September 1, 2013

12:28 a.m.–10:48 a.m.

Beloved Daughter who pointed the world to Jesus.

On the day we buried Dasah, I was fighting once again to know hope. Jesus seemed far and distant. It seemed so cruel. Where was hope? Where was God?

---

I'm so thankful our hope is not dependent
on us. Unlike with Sophie, this time my heart
was full of questions, full of anger, full of
wondering who this God I served really was.
He had revealed Himself in so many ways,
and those aspects of Him were not totally lost
to me. But for a season I questioned much of
who He was.

---

I don't remember the words Renaut spoke that day. They were heavier; there was more sorrow, more grief, and perhaps that's how it should be. Sitting in the sadness is good for the soul. Entering mourning, which is not just grief, but the expression of our grief, is difficult for our Western culture. I couldn't do anything but mourn that day.

We ended the day huddled together in front of Dasah's casket, softly singing the words to the old hymn "It Is Well with My Soul":

> When sorrows like sea billows roll,
> whatever my lot, thou hast taught me to say,
> It is well, it is well, with my soul.

I sang it through tears; I sang it in faith, for my soul did not feel well within me. And though I did not feel it at the time, I knew that God had indeed taught me to sing "when peace like a river, attendeth my way." And over the past year He had taught me to sing even when "sorrows like sea billows roll." The wellness of my soul in those moments had nothing to do with that day at the gravesite and everything to do with when the day would come "when my faith shall be sight, the clouds be rolled back as a scroll; the trump shall resound, and the Lord shall descend." Yes, that day, that day I knew it would be well with my soul.

---

She encouraged me to ask the hard questions and go to the hard places. But I was so afraid. That felt like death all over again. Would I be crying every day, all day? Would the sadness never end? Would I engage in the deep places of grief and never recover? Or worse, would I ask the hard questions of God, of myself, and discover I no longer believed He was who I thought He was?

---

But today. How could my soul be well today, when the Lord's return and heaven itself seemed so very far away? God's words would come and go in my heart, sometimes feeling empty, sometimes feeling full. More often than not it all just felt so dark and heavy. As if adding to the pain, her birth was just a week before Thanksgiving and her celebration of life was around Christmas. Holidays are hard when you've lost a loved one and more painful still when it is all so raw and fresh.

❀❀❀

A small life celebration we had put together right before Christmas held glimpses of hope, as we invited just a few people. We asked them to bring ornaments reminding them of hope and said that we would put them on our Hope tree in the window of the Hope Room as Christmas approached. I needed others to be carriers of hope for me, to remind me that we have a hope that is an anchor for our soul when my anchor felt quite dislodged.

I'm so thankful our hope is not dependent on us. Unlike with Sophie, this time my heart was full of questions, full of anger, full of wondering who this God I served really was. He had revealed Himself in so many ways, and those aspects of Him were not totally lost to me. But for a season I questioned much of who He was.

I still was struggling with the reality that God had not done what I thought He would do. I really thought He would heal Dasah, or at least He would have allowed us to bring her home. But the bigger question of my heart was why was death such a part of our story?

Where was God in all of this pain?

I opened my Bible in the months following Dasah's death, and the words fell flat. Words that had seemed to fly off the page just months before now seemed empty and void of power.

I was back and forth, up and down, struggling to accept the story God was writing for our family as right and good. I could not understand it.

The sorrow surrounded me like a heavy weight, unlike anything I had experienced after Sophie's death. My whole body shook with the agony of my empty arms. Anxiety and panic began to be a part of my daily experience. Emotions I had never experienced rose in me, and I began to fall in and out of depression. I didn't even know how to process all the pain stirring inside of me, nor did I feel I had the energy to.

It was apparent I was not in a good place just a few months after Dasah's death. My response to my grief was not only affecting me, but also affecting my marriage. Kevin continued to pursue and move toward me in his own grief, though it was often met with empty affection, empty responses. I didn't know how to change.

I knew the point of the grieving journey was not just to simply get through or get over—goodness knows I would never "get over" the loss of my children. But I needed to learn how to walk through it with greater health than I was experiencing. I began to see a counselor who became the very lifeline to the hope I needed, and I began to learn what it truly meant to lament.

I remember sitting across from my counselor, Susan, on our third appointment where most of what I did was weep uncontrollably. She had suffered deep and painful losses, and she wanted me to engage more deeply in my grief. She encouraged me to ask the hard questions and go to the hard places. But I was so afraid. That felt like death all over again. Would I be crying every day, all day? Would the sadness never end? Would I engage in the deep places of grief and never recover? Or worse, would I ask the hard questions of God, of myself, and discover I no longer believed He was who I thought He was?

C. S. Lewis put to words my fear in his book *A Grief Observed*, as he spoke of his own wrestling with God in the midst of the loss of his wife: "Not that I am (I think) in much danger of ceasing to believe in God. The real danger is of coming to believe such dreadful things about Him. The conclusion I dread is not 'So there's no God after all' but 'so this is what God is really like. Deceive yourself no longer.'"[1]

As Susan asked me to go to those deeper places of my pain, I asked her sheepishly what happened when she went to her own dark places. What happened to her faith? She smiled and through her own tears said, "I found I love Jesus more than I ever thought possible." She encouraged me to find three "Holders of Hope," safe friends who would allow me to ask the hard questions and say the hard things. Things perhaps a professing Christian dare not say out loud because of the cultural norms we've set up. And things that we too quickly try to come up with answers for or recite a pat verse over to make the listener (goodness, it certainly does not help the griever) feel better about the uneasiness of watching and hearing the deep lament of another's soul.

"God, You weren't there."

"God, You took from me, and I'm so mad at You."

"God, You feel so mean to me. Are You an absent, unkind God?"

These and more were the thoughts and feelings stirring in my heart toward God. But my "Holders of Hope" would be Susan and a few close friends who would let me grieve and lament, who would pray for me and remind me Who was the anchor for my soul. I began to feel free to mourn, free to peel back the layers of my heart that had been built up around a faulty view of God. And I began to be ready to see who He really was, however beautiful or awful it might turn out to be.

C. S. Lewis went on to say, "My idea of God is not a divine idea. It has to be shattered time after time. He shatters it Himself." My ideas of God had fallen apart over the past few years, but they had been quickly rewritten, or so I thought. This time I felt they had been utterly shattered, and I had to sit in the pieces. And in the pieces, I had to let God do the work only He could do to take Himself out of the box I didn't even know I had put Him in and show me a God I could hardly have imagined I could know.

※※※

Around this time I sat down with an old mentor, Kathryn. She lived in New Zealand and was in Orlando for a few short weeks. Every time we spent time together, it always included something fresh she learned from God's Word. That day was no different, and she opened her worn and scribbled-in Bible to Psalm 77.

---

How does one pour out the agony of their
soul freely and without constraint in a society
that frowns upon unbridled emotion?

---

She proceeded to read the words of David:

> "Will the Lord reject forever?
> And will He never be favorable again?
> Has His lovingkindness ceased forever?
> Has *His* promise come to an end forever?
> Has God forgotten to be gracious,
> Or has He in anger withdrawn His com-
> passion?" Selah.
> Then I said, "It is my grief." (vv. 7-10).

She told me that these questions were the questions of grief. And they were questions that are asked and must be asked by the grieving heart. She had written on the edge of the verses two quotes by Charles Spurgeon from his book, *The Treasury of David*, explaining further. The first said, "Each question is a dart aimed at the very heart of despair." Tears flowed as I read each question, for yes, my heart was in such despair. Spurgeon proceeds to say, "The questions are suggested by fear, but they are also the cure for fear. It is a blessed thing to have grace enough to look such questions in the face, for their answer is self-evident and eminently fitted to cheer the heart."[2]

Oh, how I wanted my heart to be cheered. Would I be courageous enough to ask these questions, truly seeking the answers and not my own preconceived notions of what I "knew" the answers were? After our time together, I decided I would do two things.

First I would buy a new Bible that would be solely for my grief work. The one I had was many years old, and it held the footprints of Sophie and Dasah. It was hard to step away from it for a season, but I knew I needed to look at God's Word afresh, with none of my markings, with no notes other than just God's Word.

I needed to wrestle.

I could not get away from what God had done and how He had already built a strong foundation of His truth in my heart in the midst of asking these questions. The questions of grief that David poses in Psalm 77 are surrounded by words that called him and us to "consider, remember and meditate" on what God had done in the past. (See verses 5-6, 11-12.)

And so the second thing I would do was take this new Bible and ask the questions David asked. I would highlight every time I saw God answer these questions and every time I saw someone ask these questions. I highlighted every time I saw anything connected to grief or mourning, and I began to search for who God really was.

Without realizing it, I was learning how to truly lament.

Lamenting is an ancient term and one that is quite foreign in our modern and fast-paced society. Dan Allender describes lament in his article "The Hidden Hope in Lament," which I discovered when I Googled "How to Lament." Googling is not always something I would recommend; Kevin highly discourages the habit I have for Googling things. But I did not understand how to lament and had heard no one talk about it.

How does one pour out the agony of their soul freely and without constraint in a society that frowns upon unbridled emotion? We give people a few weeks, maybe a month or two to grieve the loss of a loved one, and then we are surprised when we discover they are still wrestling deeply.

---

I wanted to get away, I wanted to have reason
to turn from my God who didn't function like
I thought He would. Instead, I was drawn in.

---

And then it happens to us, and we, too, are surprised when months and even years go by and our hearts are crying out to be free—to cry out.

We like happy thoughts and sending good vibes (whatever that means), and someone please tell me, "It's all going to be OK." We like music that doesn't feel too sad for too long. And when we are grieving, we are just waiting for the day when we won't feel so very sad. But what if feeling the gravitas of our pain, the pain of our brothers and sisters, is good for the soul? What if it actually enables us to experience the groan of all creation that Paul speaks of and to long for heaven that much more?

What Allender said in his article on lament struck me:

> Christians seldom sing in the minor key. We fear the somber; we seem to hold sorrow in low esteem. We seem predisposed to fear lament as a quick slide into doubt and despair, failing to see that doubt and despair are the dark soil that is necessary to grow confidence and joy.
>
> Consider how many times you have heard another person encourage a struggling believer (perhaps, you): "It doesn't help to get upset, you simply need to trust the Lord." The assumption is that trust precludes struggle; faith erases doubt; hope removes despair. Therefore, lament is unnecessary if one trusts, loves, and obeys God.
>
> Sadly, we have misunderstood the great value of public and private lament. To lament—that is, to cry out to God with our doubts, our incriminations of him and others, to bring a complaint against him—is the context for surrender. Surrender—the turning of our heart over to him, asking for mercy, and receiving his terms for restoration—is impossible without battle. To put it simply, it is inconceivable to surrender to God unless there is a prior, declared war against him. . . .
>
> It is crucial to comprehend a lament is as far from complaining or grumbling as a search is from aimless

wandering. A grumbler has already reached a conclusion, shut down all desire, and postures with questions that are barely concealed accusations. . . .

A person who laments may sound like a grumbler—both vocalize anguish, anger, and confusion. But a lament involves even deeper emotion because a lament is truly asking, seeking, and knocking to comprehend the heart of God. A lament involves the energy to search, not to shut down the quest for truth. It is passion to ask, rather than to rant and rave with already reached conclusions. A lament uses the language of pain, anger, and confusion and moves toward God.[3]

During this season of learning to lament, my college friends, who presumptuously and affectionately call ourselves the "Red Brick Hotties" or RBH Ladies for short, gathered for a reunion we try to have every few years. They wanted to surround me with love and encouragement as I was in my most broken season.

I was so thankful for this, but to be honest I did not know how to bring the full extent of my brokenness to them. And I'm not sure they knew how to engage with me in my pain either. We gathered at a large beach house off the coast of North Carolina. It was at the end of February, just three months after Dasah had died.

Each day I would take my music and Bible and walk down the beach, letting the tears fall in a time and space where no one could see or hear. I realized as I walked that the fog was so heavy, the beach so empty, and the sound of the waves so loud that if I screamed no one would hear. So I began to do that each day, to wail at the waves of my pain.

> Every step revealed more of Him—in community, in loneliness, and in grief. In my waiting, my suffering, and my surrender, every time He had given more of Himself.

One of those mornings I was having another lamenting session at the edge of the water when I decided to let out more of my anger toward the waves. I picked up shells, rocks, anything I could find. I released my anger toward God and my questions with each shell and rock. I wanted to hear something crack or break, but I could hardly see the rocks even make a splash in the roaring waves as I hurled each question toward God.

Where *were* You?

Where *are* You?

Do You *see* me?

Why did I have to lose one, much less *two* babies?

It's so *unfair*. Are You a *mean* God?

And the waves kept coming.

Are You a *cruel* God?

I visualized an image of my Savior on the cross.

You don't *feel* near.

And the waves kept coming.

You don't *feel* loving.

And I could see the nails in His hands. And the waves kept coming. Calling me, beckoning me, reminding me how deep my Father's love was for me.

I wanted to get away, I wanted to have reason to turn from my God who didn't function like I thought He would. Instead, I was drawn in to the steady and consistent crashing of the waves, moving closer as each shell found its mark, who knows where, enveloped by the sea. And so was I.

I was drawn in to the steady crashing of the waves of His love that made as much sense as the vastness of the ocean, my questions enveloped by His mighty power.

I was small, weak, and my utter humanity and finiteness were awakened at the edge of the sea. The vastness before me.

---

### And in the depth of the pain I brought to Him, He reminded me of the pain He bore for me.

---

Alone.

It was God and me and the sea before me.

I couldn't see more than a hundred yards, surrounded by mist, surrounded by mystery.

I knew what was beyond the mist. More sea.

Did I know that beyond what I could see of God there was more of Him to be seen?

Had I not learned this in the entirety of the past three years?

Every step revealed more of Him—in community, in loneliness, and in grief. In my waiting, my suffering, and my surrender, every time He had given more of Himself.

I lost sight of this so quickly. I could continue to clench my hands and run, or release them and fall to my knees.

His ways were higher, His understanding greater. And oh, the greatness of His love that extended beyond what I could even dare to comprehend.

The lament of my heart brought me to surrender, and the surrender made my heart dance, and then my feet quite literally found a new song.

It was a song of freedom, my surrender to the One I could trust, the One who is Lord over all; He is worthy of my praise and worship.

My questions fell unanswered at His feet, swallowed up by the sea, swallowed up by His love. I was met instead by the realization that the God of the universe who didn't have to tolerate my questions, who didn't have to envelop me in my sorrow, continued to draw near to me.

I was wrecked, I was broken, and for perhaps the first time I felt free.

I crumpled on the beach as I looked out at the waves, seeing none of the rocks or shells I had hurled with every ounce of strength in me. I realized that God was like the waves that just kept coming for me. He kept coming for me. He was not fazed at all by my questions or by my pain. In those questions God continued to remind me of His love and His grace. And in the depth of the pain I brought to Him, He reminded me of the pain He bore for me.

My questions were stilled in a way they had not been before as I sat there thinking of my Savior, thinking of the vastness of the ocean and the vastness of my God. *MY God.* Yes, He is my God, the one who would draw near to me *in the midst* of my questions, not when I stopped having them.

He is the One who wanted to reveal Himself to me so that I would lose all my preconceived notions of who I thought He was and see Him for who He really is.

I looked to my left as I bent down low and saw a shell, a single shell filled with water, sitting peacefully just above the edge of the rolling waves. And I was reminded of a quote I had always loved: "Lose your life, give it up. Can the shell give up the teaspoon of water it holds lest there not be enough in the ocean to fill it? Can you and I imagine the depth and plenitude of God's love?"[4]

Could I trust that in giving up myself, in losing myself to the One who had given Himself for me, I might in fact discover that He is indeed not who I thought He was—He's better?

*He's better.*

His ways did not make sense to me that day on the beach where the fog surrounded me, but something began to switch inside of me. My mourning quite literally began to turn to dancing. I began to dance in reckless abandon, uncoordinated and sloppy rhythmic moves, skipping along the beach as I listened to music of His grace and mercy.

Oh, how He loves me. Oh, how He comes for me. Oh, how my questions are stilled at the foot of the cross. My questions are still there but stilled for those sweet moments.

I still felt the sorrow, pain, and weight of losing two children. My heart was still filled with grief, but in the releasing of the question of "why" I began to slowly discover the hope of knowing the answer to "Who?" This God I could not begin to comprehend, I knew if nothing else, He suffered with me and loved me with an everlasting love.

That weekend as I began to release my pain to God, receiving His love in fresh and transformational ways, I was able to bring that pain to my friends who had gathered around me. More deeply secure in the love of the Father, I was able to receive more fully the love from the women He had chosen to put in my life to gather around me, weep, and mourn with me.

God continued to meet me in my questions as I learned to lament and ask questions with a posture toward Him. I truly wanted to know and hear how He wanted to respond. My posture in my pain was toward God. I continued to search out honestly who God was in His Word, and my heart began to slowly, ever so slowly, like Spurgeon said of those questions David asked, be cheered. And Hope, the Hope that doesn't disappoint when "all around my soul gives way" became more firmly written on my heart.[5]

God wasn't who I thought He was. He was so much better.

Beginning to learn how to lament was drawing me to a deeper awe of God than I had ever known and a deeper surrender to His story for my life.

# TWENTY

## The Unimaginable Hope

*All suffering, all pain, all emptiness, all disappointment is seed:*
*sow it in God and he will, finally, bring a crop of joy from it.*

—Eugene Peterson

Seven months after Dasah died, grief was still heavy on my heart, but a fresh hope and perspective were rising. I'd spent much of those seven months resisting that this was the story God had written for our lives. The lament of my soul continued to surface the question, "Why would God allow such chapters to be woven into our lives?" I understood intellectually that I could not change our story. I had carried Sophie in my belly for forty-two weeks and two days, and she lived for ten hours, and then she had died. That was a fact I could not change, and in some strange place in my heart I had accepted that fact. Sophie's story was a beautiful, albeit painful, story for me.

But Dasah's story was, well, another story altogether. Where Sophie's life revealed how much God had done in our lives to keep us tightly woven with Him on our journey with her amid the pain, Dasah's life ripped at the very seams of my faith.

Yes, it was a fact that fourteen months after burying our firstborn daughter, we walked through carrying another child, discovering she would not live, and then burying her next to her sister. And I resisted that this was Dasah's story, for somehow I thought if I accepted it, I was saying it was right and good. And that, I felt ill-equipped to do. A phrase from an Amy Carmichael poem came to mind "In acceptance lieth peace."[1] I needed that peace, for surely I was still struggling to experience peace.

&#x2756;&#x2756;&#x2756;

My husband and I were taking classes on things like the theology of salvation and humanity and the history of the church that summer after Dasah's death. In between all of the intellectualism and heady words, sitting in each class took on a whole new meaning for me than classes like these I had taken before.

Perhaps it's because the things we learned mattered more to me.

My professor of church history began each class singing a cappella old hymns I had never heard. I think he assumed we knew the words to these hymns, or else wanted to make sure we learned them. Everyone seemed to catch on to the lyrics and tunes quickly. It was probably not the environment most worship leaders in the church of our culture would say would draw people into intimate worship, but each morning as I followed along with the words on the screen, hearing the sound of the one hundred plus students echoing off the walls of the large classroom, led by the old and seasoned professor with the booming but slightly off-key voice, tears formed in my eyes.

There was something raw and vulnerable and real about those moments, singing words that radiated the rich and deep truths of God. Every morning God met me there as class began.

For all the pages of books we read, I discovered truths of who God is that mattered far more than being able to regurgitate knowledge on a test or in ministry. No, I sat in each class, my eyes and ears attuned to everything the professors said—searching, waiting, and eager to hear what truths God Himself would rewrite on my heart.

I say rewrite for I saw in my lack of peace my unwillingness to fully receive and, yes, even embrace the story God had for us, an incomplete and even wrongly perceived view of God.

And wasn't my prayer long ago to truly know God no matter the cost?

Yes, this was what He was doing. In all the pain and all the joys of the past several years, He was peeling back everything my heart believed about Him that was not true and was ever so slowly in His steadfast and patient way, replacing it with what was true of Him.

Was He still the same good and faithful and loving Father I declared with boldness He was just a couple of years earlier?

Had His character changed when my circumstances seemed to get worse instead of better?

Would I still trust Him with the pen of my story even when it made little sense?

Accepting this story for our lives was not ultimately saying it was right and good that my daughters died. Death is the enemy, and death is what Christ came to defeat and conquer, which He did. And though death still is a part of our lives, Christ promises that one day death itself will be the last enemy to die, completely and forever.

No. Accepting it was saying He was right and good in all He did, in all He allowed in His ultimate and infinite sovereignty—even if I could not comprehend how these aspects of His character fit together.

One day while in a café, I was processing many of these thoughts with God. I was about to speak to another woman (whom I had not yet met) who just received the same diagnosis for her child that we received for Dasah. What should she do? How could she walk this path? These were all questions she would no doubt ask, and how was I to respond? Every woman I met who faced the same situation processed it differently. Every person grieves differently. I could not anticipate what she would need, so I prayed instead that the Holy Spirit would give me words that would speak to her heart, words only He knew she needed to hear—much like others had done for us. In those moments, all I thought was how much I needed to hear from God in my own wrestling.

While waiting for that conversation, words flowed from the depths of my heart onto paper. I wrote furiously with a deeper conviction than I had known before. I put words to the emotions of all my fears in accepting this story as my own—words that I first shared with this woman. She would go on to choose life for her child and find a fresh hope in her own season of grief and joy.

I realized in this season of lament that just like Job, "I spoke of things I did not understand, things too wonderful for me. . . . My ears had heard of you but now my eyes have seen you. Therefore . . . I repent" (Job 42:3, 5-6 NIV).

Yes, in this season, I was and still am wrestling, and the wrestle has enabled me to see God in ways I had never known but so longed for.

---

I had given God my pain in this season of love and loss, and He had given me so much more in return. Himself. And I realized that all along, He was who I wanted.

---

I wrote that day:

> Lord, If I could have more of You and lose my daughters or less of You and keep them, I don't know what I would choose. If I knew the tastes of glory I would see through the short lives they would receive, would I have said yes to this story more quickly years ago? I truly don't know, for I want them back so much.
>
> I want a different story so badly.

But a different story would be two different little girls and less of You.

And I want the more of You part and the two little girls You gave me. I do not wish that death invaded my life so abruptly, so painfully, but if this is the way to You, if this is the way to know, to taste Your glory, Your majesty, then I receive it. With arms wide open and tears of joy mixed with pain running down my cheeks and breaths of hope mingled with often suffocating loss.

So be it.

No, not only so be it . . . but a resounding YES, LORD.

Yes to the story You have chosen for our lives. For my life. For Sophie's life. For Dasah's life. I do not understand it. I do not claim to know the depth of Your ways or the greatness of Your love in this story, but I know it is intertwined throughout.

I would not trade my story for another, for in doing so I would lose so much. Perhaps it would seem I have already lost so much. "But whatever things were gain to me, those things I have counted as loss for the sake of Christ. More than that, I count all things to be loss in view of the surpassing value of knowing Christ Jesus my Lord" (Philippians 3:7-8).

This I know, that today, I love You more than I did three years ago. But more than that, today Your greatness, Your glory, Your profound worthiness of my life is both more a mystery and more clear at the same time. Your holiness has been revealed to me in ways I never knew. Your greatness at the cross is clearer because the reality of the tomb being empty is more profound.

> *Life has won.*
> *Death is defeated.*
> *And You, Lord, have become my greatest hope.*
> *Yes. Yes to Your ways, for Your ways are good*
> *and right, and even in death Your ways lead to*
> *life.*

I had given God my pain in this season of love and loss, and He had given me so much more in return. Himself. And I realized that all along, He was who I wanted.

❈❈❈

I could not have known or comprehended that around the time those words were penned more on my heart than a page, a little boy was being conceived whose brave momma, nine months later, would make an adoption plan for him and choose us to be his parents.

---

It is tempting to believe after significant loss
that gain is proof of God's goodness. It is
hard to imagine that His goodness resides in
both loss and gain.

---

I could not have known that as I sit today at the coffee shop Kevin and I would go to after every doctor's appointment with Sophie, taking a much-needed break to write and meet with God, that Kevin would be at home with our now almost-six-month-old son, Jaden.

Today, as I write, we are approaching what would be Sophie's third birthday and three months later, Dasah's second birthday. I could not have known that, though the ache is still deep, the laughter and joy would be slowly restored.

I am hesitant to even share of our adoption of a son lest you are tempted to think all is well and has been redeemed.

It has not.

If it had, we would have no need for hope. For as the apostle Paul says, "But hope that is seen is no hope at all. Who hopes for what they already have? But if we hope for what we do not yet have, we wait for it patiently" (Romans 8:24-25 NIV).

The hope that doesn't disappoint, the hope we are waiting for with patience, the hope being forged in our hearts is not in earthly things but in the One who sits at the right hand of the throne of God. Jesus.

Our Hope is in a person, the person of Jesus Christ.

And *that* Hope will never disappoint. Why? Paul also says the progression of suffering produces endurance, which produces character, which produces hope that does not disappoint because "God's love has been poured into our hearts through the Holy Spirit who has been given to us" (Romans 5:5 ESV).

What love has been poured out but the growing understanding of "the love of Christ that surpasses knowledge" (Ephesians 3:19 ESV). And what happens when we know that love? We are "filled with all the fullness of God" (Ephesians 3:19 ESV). And how do we know this love? Through the working of the Holy Spirit in our lives in the midst of every circumstance. My circumstances have disappointed me, but my God who came down in the form of man to pay the penalty for my sins to give me life and hope (both now and for eternity) has never disappointed me.

He is the One who is the Author and Perfecter of our faith—the One holding us with His unfailing love. He is the One who has come, His life redeeming our lives now and pointing us to the promise of that glorious day when He will come again and redeem everything in full.

It is tempting to believe after significant loss that gain is proof of God's goodness. It is hard to imagine that His goodness resides in both loss and gain.

But it is the goodness of the pain of the cross that makes the goodness of the joy of the resurrection that much more good. And because of the cross I was reminded in the weeks after Jaden's arrival that he was not proof of God's goodness to us, but a reminder that God is good in all things.

The evidence of God's goodness is found on the cross. What more do we need to know and see to be convinced that our God is a good and loving God? There is no greater love than this, no greater demonstration of goodness than that our God would take on the sin of mankind so that we could have life. And this is what He does.

He gives life in death and life in life.

He brings joy in mourning and joy in rejoicing.

It is His presence where true joy and true hope are found. And it has been His presence that Kevin and I have come to delight in more fully, more deeply in the past several years.

That first week home, with Jaden in my arms, I was surprised I did not experience an overwhelming sense of God's goodness in a child we got to parent and finally bring home. It felt strange.

What I did experience was an overwhelming sense of awe and wonder at God's ways, for truly I did not believe we would bring home a child so quickly after entering the adoption process. It was a profound moment, for I realized I wasn't more convinced of God's goodness. I did not need the Lord to provide a child in our arms to convince me of His goodness and His worthiness in my life.

I was already convinced.

Those truths had been rooting themselves in my heart over three years, in the valley of the shadow of death. And in the darkness of the valley was where I wrestled and discovered the Lord, faithful and good.

Today, His faithfulness, His goodness is in bringing new life into our home and giving us the privilege of learning to parent Jaden. The past three years, His faithfulness, His goodness has been giving us two little girls to parent for a short amount of time and walking us through deep loss.

I cannot predict what His faithfulness will be tomorrow, but I know He will be faithful. I know He will be good. For God is at work causing

"ALL THINGS to work together for good to those who love God, to those who are called according to His purpose" (Romans 8:28, emphasis mine) R. C. Sproul powerfully sheds light on this passage:

> This verse is not merely a biblical expression of comfort for those who suffer affliction. It is far more than that. It is a radical credo for the Christian worldview. It represents the absolute triumph of divine purpose over all alleged acts of chaos. It erases "misfortune" from the vocabulary of the Christian.
>
> God, in his providence, has the power and the will to work all things together for good for his people. This does not mean that everything that happens to us is, in itself, good. Really bad things do happen to us. But . . . they are bad only in the short (proximate) term, never in the long term. Because of the triumph of God's goodness in all things, he is able to bring good for us out of the bad. He turns our tragedies into supreme blessings.[2]

❀❀❀

Nineteen years ago, when I entered my first year of college, I began to pray that I would know Jesus in the way Paul did when he says to the people of Philippi, "I count all things to be loss in view of the surpassing value of knowing Christ Jesus my Lord" (Philippians 3:8). I prayed that I, too, would be willing to lose it all just to know Him, knowing how worthy He really is. I could not have comprehended at the young age of nineteen how God would become more than knowledge in my head but the experience of my soul. And I could not have known that He would answer that prayer as I waited on Him, suffered with Him, and surrendered to Him. This has been, and no doubt will continue to be, a daily experience. For "one does not surrender a life in an instant. That which is lifelong can only be surrendered in a lifetime."[3]

There will be new joys and no doubt new heartaches to come. We live in a fallen world. None of us is exempt from the effects of the fall. But as we press into God in the pain and in the joy, He is strengthening in us a kind of trust in Him that will hold us in the present joys and the future uncertainties. And it is Christ who does the work, through the incredible power of His Spirit.

What kind of hope are you tethering yourself to today? What new strands of God's trustworthiness, His character, need to be more tightly bound in your heart? There will always be new aspects of God's character to cling to more tightly, for who can measure the depths of God?

---

I can live in hope at the grave of my own buried dreams because today God has breathed His resurrection hope and life into the crevices of my pain.

---

"For now we see in a mirror dimly, but then face-to-face. Now I know in part; then I shall know fully, even as I have been fully known" (1 Corinthians 13:12 ESV).

Today is not the day for seeing fully but for knowing more and more in part the great riches of the Lord that led Paul to say and countless others to repeat as prayers of their heart: "Oh Lord, to know you . . . just to know you, just to share in your sufferings, just to get to plumb the depths of your love, I would lose it all if I could just know you" (Philippians 3:7-10, paraphrase).

Must it require such loss? No and yes. We need not go looking to lose those things most precious to us; but we must ask the question, "Are the things we hold most precious and long for the most surrendered to Christ?"

"He who has found his life will lose it, and he who has lost his life for My sake will find it" (Matthew 10:39).

We lose our lives when we discover that which we are holding onto that is ultimately insecure and unstable.

We lose our lives when we say, "I'll do it Your way and not my way, Lord."

We lose our lives when we surrender our ideas for how our story will unfold to His ways.

We give Him every dream, we say "It's Yours, do with it as You wish," and we watch God give us new dreams, dreams we never knew we wanted and dreams that redeem the ones broken by pain.

All you need to do is come. Bring your broken, bring your tears, bring your disappointment, bring your questions, and surrender. God has met me in the waiting, in the suffering, and in my daily surrender. These are the places He has forged and is continuing to forge in me the kind of Hope that doesn't disappoint.

And these are the places God will forge it in you.

These are the places your buried dreams will lead you to—the Resurrection Hope that extends beyond ourselves, straight to the cross, then to the grave, and then to the right hand of our heavenly Father. Sorrow and suffering can be transformed in your heart (as it has in mine) to joy and peace. The beauty of what Christ has done for me has been discovered in the sorrow, and the glory of Christ has been magnified in my suffering.

I can live in hope at the grave of my own buried dreams because today God has breathed His resurrection hope and life into the crevices of my pain.

Must it have taken the death of my first two daughters? Could there not have been another way? I do not know the answer to those questions, but I do know the One who holds the answers to those questions. And today I am a little more quick than I was a few years ago to say, like Jesus, "yet not My will, but Yours be done" (Luke 22:42).

I long to have Sophie, Dasah, and Jaden together in our arms, in our home. But there would be no Jaden without Dasah. And there would be no Dasah without Sophie. And there would not be the depth of awe and wonder and adoration I have for my King without the children God has given us, without the stories God has written for us and is continuing to unveil to us.

Each of the chapters in our stories is marked by joy and pain. And in each of these chapters we pray God will continue to reveal His mighty power to redeem, His overwhelming goodness, His never-ending love, and that we have a Hope who is the anchor for our soul. Sure and steadfast.

So we sit as believers in the wonders of the Kingdom come as we groan for the Kingdom coming. And we know that every buried dream will not remain in ashes, for that day more than two thousand years ago, everything changed for us.

It is because of the resurrection that five years ago the transforming power of Christ began to bring joy in the midst of pain, hope in the midst of sorrow, and life in the midst of death. Jesus changes everything, and for our little family of five, when death invaded our world, the transforming power of Christ invaded it more.

*We see not yet all things put under Thee.*
*We see not yet the glory that shall be;*
*We see not yet, and yet by faith we see;*
*Alleluia, Alleluia.*

*We see the shadows gathering for flight,*
*The powers of dawn dispel the brooding night,*
*The steadfast march of the triumphant light;*
*Alleluia.*

*Be we in East or West, or North or South,*
*By wells of water or in land of drouth,*
*Lo, Thou hast put a new song in our mouth;*
*Alleluia.*

*Therefore we triumph; therefore we are strong,*
*Though vision tarry and the night be long;*
*For lifted up, we conquer by Thy song;*
*Alleluia.*

—Amy Carmichael,
"We Conquer by His Song"

# EPILOGUE

## A Note from Sophie and Dasah's Dad

As you've journeyed through this book—and the words of my amazing wife—you've gotten to know us as a family, and even more specifically you've gotten to know our precious daughters, Sophie and Dasah. I experience incredible delight welling up inside of me as their dad as someone gets to meet, cherish, and be influenced by our children.

While you weren't there in the hospital room to meet our daughters in person, as you've walked these preceding pages it's as if you were there with us in some way getting to soak in the chubby little cheeks of Sophie, relishing in the sounds of Dasah's sweet little voice, and tenderly holding them as they stretched and wiggled. Words cannot adequately capture the joy it brings me as their dad that through this book you've gotten to meet our daughters. One of the great heartaches on the days they were born was that more people weren't able to meet them. Yet throughout our pregnancies with them, and as we've gotten to share through words and photos after they went to be with Jesus, many more have gotten to meet our daughters. And that's what brings such joy to a parent: introducing the world to those who are most precious to them.

But there is something that makes me even more proud as their dad.

In getting to meet our daughters, you've also gotten to know our great God a little more, perhaps even be introduced to Him for the first time. Our greatest desire is that each of our children would intimately know our glorious God, and even more so, that God would enable others to know Him through their lives. He is the very definition of love and the One whom life—in all its fullness and depth—is found. And what is astounding is that in Sophie and Dasah's short time here on this earth, more people came to see and know God afresh than those Lindsey and I have influenced in our years of life combined.

And my life was by all means one of those. We have and continue to journey through grief together as a family, and while Lindsey and I walk alongside each other, we think and feel and experience the journey differently. And in that, God leads and cares for us differently. Thus, the ways in which knowing God for me has deepened over these years have come in different ways and at different times than what you've just gotten to read from my wife. This has certainly been true as He has transformed my hope in Him over these years of being a dad.

When we found out about Sophie's diagnosis, it was absolutely devastating, but neither Lindsey nor I ever wrestled much with the "why" questions of God. I did not understand why our first daughter had anencephaly, but honestly the need to understand wasn't heavy on my heart. But as we walked with Dasah in pregnancy, the questions of "why?!" and wanting to understand what in the world God was doing were far more important than they ever were with Sophie.

In the days that followed Dasah's diagnosis, the first passage I found God leading me to was Psalm 42:5, which says, "Why are you cast down, O my soul, and why are you in turmoil within me? Hope in God; for I shall again praise him, my salvation" (ESV).

As I read over it again and again, I knew why my soul was cast down. There was no question about that. But I was struck anew by the command to "hope in God." I was realizing I really didn't know what that meant.

What does it look like to truly find my hope in God alone? Not hope in what I think He will do, or how I think He will benefit me. But to simply have hope in who He is. At a time when I needed hope, it did not seem like an ideal time to see my foundation of hope being changed. So we began to pray every day that God would teach us what it means for our hope, joy, and faith to be firmly planted in who He is.

As the months passed and we continued to pray, God used His Word and the words of authors of various books to unearth some of the roots of where my hope was found. As we had walked with Sophie, I had great hope that God would heal our daughter, but I knew that God was God (and I was not), and it was up to Him and according to His bigger, sovereign plans if Sophie would be healed. I had peace in His sovereignty regardless of what He chose. But I also had great hope that God would give us more children in the future that would be fully healthy and remain on this earth with us for decades to come.

And while I had never articulated it in words—even to myself—I believed God would never have us walk through the same grievous journey with any of our other children. How could He?! That would not be the redemption and silver lining that I was longing for, hoping for—and not just hoping for, but hoping in. In my mind, my hope was of course in God, but more specifically in what God would do—that He would give us future healthy children that we would get to parent and watch grow up.

And so when we discovered our second daughter was also diagnosed with a terminal condition, it felt even more devastating and heavy than Sophie's diagnosis. This wasn't how the story was supposed to go! How could our God of redemption and restoration write a story like this?! I was now questioning how to find hope in God because He hadn't come through as I was certain He would. And as I dug into this angst in my heart, God began to give me a deeper look at where my hope "in Him" truly was. Not in Him, but in what I thought He should or would do. I was at a loss.

So I began to pray He would teach me and enable me to have hope securely in who He is, and not in my current or future hoped-for circumstances. Months went by, and while I didn't often feel this deep intimacy with God, He had been showing me much about Him and myself and the brokenness of our world. I continued to pray that He would teach me to truly hope in Him, not knowing what that really looked like. I was driving home a few weeks before Dasah was born—after a time of journaling, reading, talking with God, and listening to Him—and seemingly out of nowhere, it hit me.

Over the months God had been teaching me what it looked like to hope in Him—and I didn't even realize it. I didn't realize it largely because I was looking for a "hopeful" feeling, a comforting sort of warmth inside my heart (my wife could probably do a much better job putting words to these emotions). But God was teaching me not about a comforting feeling. He was teaching me that hope was found in knowing Him, in knowing His character, and in trusting Him because I knew Him.

I know that He is good.

I know that He is loving, and that He loves me, and Lindsey, and Sophie, and Dasah, more than I even have the capacity to understand.

I know He is righteous.

I know He is powerful.

I know He knows all things, knows the much bigger story on an eternal scale, and He is in total control of this story—His story.

I can thus trust Him with the life of my daughters and my wife and my own life. I can trust Him with the story of our family. And as I get to know more and more the One who I am trusting in these things, I have great hope.

Nancy Guthrie writes in a wonderful book on grief, "The truth is, we're often more interested in getting what God's got—not getting more of God. . . . But God knows exactly what we need, and His purposes are grander than giving us what we want. He's doing something deeper."[1]

I saw this in myself. As I would get glimpses of what it looked like to truly hope in God, I still often just wanted God to give me what I wanted. I wanted to be God instead of trusting God.

But when I stepped back from my immediate feelings and momentary circumstances, I really did believe God's bigger story is so much better. It's a story that is eternal (and not just about the immediate pages ahead that I couldn't see). It's a story centered not on me, or my family, but on Him because He is the one that we were designed to know and to be fulfilled in knowing Him. It's a story of deep sadness, deep heartache, and also deep joy (and not just for us, but God also). It's a story of greater redemption on an eternal scale. But finally, Romans 8:32 reminds us, "He who did not spare his own Son but gave him up for us all, how will he not also with him graciously give us all things?" (ESV) Because of God sending Jesus to live, suffer, and die alongside us and for us, this story God was writing in our family was a story of hope. Our great God was not withholding anything from us so that we might suffer. Our God has given everything—even the life of His only son—so that we could know Him, now and for eternity. In Him and simply who He is, I was learning to find great hope.

As parents, our children continually teach us many things. This was one of the greatest things my daughters Sophie and Dasah pointed me to. It was something only God could reveal about Himself, but he chose to allow my daughters to be part of it. Perhaps He is allowing them to be part of some of the ways He is revealing Himself to you.

It brings me great pride as a dad to know they're part of such priceless work.

# ACKNOWLEDGMENTS

I did not set out to write a book when I began my blog nearly six years ago now. In fact as the thought crossed my mind and then continued to become more than a thought but a desire to pursue, I didn't know the first thing about writing a book. So many people have pushed and encouraged me along the way that I cannot help but be overwhelmed with gratitude for those who have helped to make this book you are holding in your hands a reality.

First, to my husband, Kevin. There are no words to express how grateful I am for your support on this journey of both living and writing this story. You have pointed me to the Rock over and over in the midst of my wavering faith. You are my fearless leader, friend, companion, and love of my life. I'm sure both of us wondered when we invested in that online course to learn how to write a book if it would come to anything or just be another crazy idea I had that I wouldn't follow through on! But you have been relentlessly encouraging, and I could not have written this without you. You have reminded me countless times in the writing and rewriting that you believed in not only me, but what God had to say through me even in times when I didn't and wondered if this was really a good idea, wanting to toss the manuscript out the window. Thank you for not letting me give up or toss out the manuscript and for being my greatest champion on this endeavor. It may just say my name on the cover, but we did this together. This story is not just mine, but ours. And you gave me courage to see it to completion. As we said in our vows, "and as a family, we will serve each other and the world with the gospel of Jesus Christ," may this book be a piece of many pieces to come of the fulfillment of that vow.

To Jaden, my son. Thank you for taking long naps so I could write and for just bringing so much joy to my life. Thank you for being such a beautiful reminder of God's grace and love. I love being your mommy!

To Briella, my daughter. I can't believe I got to bring you home. Carrying you and birthing you while finishing this book has been both a sweet gift and a fresh reminder of the truths I've needed to hold onto, as I trust God with your life.

To Jordan McKinney, thank you for offering to watch and love on Jaden in those early stages of writing!

To Sarah Humphrey, thank you for your belief that I could even write a book, enough to connect me with your editor, not even knowing I was in the midst of writing a book at the time. Your encouragement was truly a catalyst to seeing this book published when I didn't know the first thing about publishing!

To Dawn Woods, the first editor who graciously looked at an incredibly unprofessional pitch and believed in this story enough to stay with me and encourage me to fine-tune a book proposal and be willing to consider pitching it to your publisher. You pitched it and championed it to Abingdon Press and then became my official editor. Truly, I am so grateful for you. Thank you for all the work you put into editing this book, making suggestions, encouraging me in my writing, and enabling this book to be what it is today!

To Susan Cornell, Susan Salley, Brenda Smotherman, and the Abingdon Press team, thank you for investing in this book, for taking a risk with a new author and allowing me the privilege to be a part of the Abingdon Press community. I am so grateful for each of you and the work you have done in marketing, design, publishing, and answering every one of my countless questions along the way!

To my Mom, Jennafer White, Emily Weller, Chris Rule, and Adrienne Minor. You were my first editors before I had to turn in a presentable manuscript to Abingdon Press. The fact that you braved a manuscript that was twice as long and infinitely messier speaks volumes to me! Your feedback and encouragement was invaluable.

Adrienne, I must single you out because you went above and beyond helping to edit down, rearrange, and reword and basically made editing your second job without pay. This book would not be what it is without you! Also, thank you for helping me increase my vocabulary!

To my parents, Mike and Tracey Parrott, I'm so grateful to have parents who have rooted me in God's Word and truth, prayed relentlessly for me in every season of my life, and navigated these deep waters of grief with me. Thank you for encouraging me throughout the process—Mom, for helping me fine-tune my book proposal and reminding me often of why I wrote this in the first place (especially when I was struggling and unsure of whether or not it even made sense!), and Dad, for helping make sure it was all theologically sound.

To my siblings—Luke Parrott, Laurie Schultz, Dan Parrott, my brother-in-law, Nick Schultz, and my sister-in-law, Mandy Parrott—I'm not sure how I got so lucky to have such incredibly supportive siblings, but you have loved and encouraged us through the darkest times, and I wish I could have told every story in this book of how each of you has come alongside of us over the last five years.

To the family I married into, Michael and Mayra Dennis, David and Laura Dennis, and especially my mother- and father-in-law, Kathy and Jim Dennis. Kathy and Jim, you have loved me like your own daughter through the darkness and encouraged me in the healing and now the writing of this book. Thank you!

To Jessica Bott and Julie Kwon, our weekly process group was invaluable to me in a season of deep pain, and your presence with me on this journey gave me courage to press into my pain and trust God in new and fresh ways. Julie, thank you for fighting for our friendship in the midst of both of us giving birth to little girls around the same time and being gracious, loving, and truthful to me as we navigated that. I'm grateful for your encouragement and support and nearly fifteen years of friendship. Also, electric toothbrushes.

To Elyse South, Jennafer White, and Katie Reed, your willingness to engage your hearts and allow my pain to become your pain has been a balm to my soul. Thank you for loving our family, for encouraging me in writing, and for being willing to engage in the messiness of grief with me.

To Susan Larrett, my counselor, my holder of hope, the one who gave me a vision of what it could be like to know Jesus in the midst of the storm of my grief. The fact that I could be in a place to write the words in this book is a testimony to really good counseling, a gracious God, and God using you in my life to unlock places of pain and move my heart toward God and not away. Thank you.

To Nancy Guthrie, thank you for offering your own pain and loss that others would see God's healing power. I remember being pregnant with Dasah as you spoke at a conference and opened with a song. I thought then if God could enable you to sing after losing two children, perhaps He could give me a new song too. Thank you for your Respite Retreat Ministry and willingness to engage with me on my journey. Your books and journey have propelled me forward on my own. And this book is a part of the new song He has put on my heart.

To Amanda Kern and Scott Taylor with Now I Lay Me Down to Sleep, your presence in the most beautiful and broken moments of our lives captured not only photos but memories that have helped me remember vividly moments that have become more cloudy in my mind over the years. Thank you for being available and for NILMDTS for offering such a beautiful service for families like ours. I was able to recall those memories in writing much more authentically in this book because of those photos!

To the Red Brick Hotties—Amanda Epting, Elizabeth Cullen, Bethany Hoang, Bethany Buckner, Jill Klaiber, Jess Anderson, Anne Handy, Jennifer Colaner, Andrea Fuderer, Bonnie Yelverton and Alisha Bauer—you each have modeled such grace and love to me, even from afar, and have continually encouraged me in so many unique ways. Those few days on the beach in North Carolina were life-changing, and I'm so thankful to have friends like you.

To my Supporting C.A.S.T., all those near and far and many whose names I do not know. Thank you for coming alongside us, and thank you Mosaic Church for your generous support and encouragement and rallying around us as a community through the darkness. Renaut and Brooke Van Der Riet, Jennafer and Brady White, Elyse and Mac South, Brandon and Katie Reed, Holly and Lynn Gallagher, Carrie Waters, Jennafer Newberry, Emily Mills, and every single other person a part of this story. I wish I could write pages of each of your names. But know that I am so grateful for each of you.

To my coworkers over the years—Kristel Pendergrass, Cate and Brandon Powell, Adrienne Minor, Nick and Alicia Keswani, Josh and Maddie Fieleke, Sarah and Aaron Emerson, Julie and Danny Kwon, thank you for navigating this journey with us, for giving us space, adding at times more work to your own plate and being present with us through the joy and pain. Thank you for the gift of your presence on this journey.

And to all the staff who cared for us at Florida Hospital—Dr. Kjeuroff, Dr. Al-Mahlt, Robyn, Marie, Stacey, Doreen, Sarah, Lauren, Tracey, Lynn, Toni, Tori, Minnie, Jennifer, Kendall, and the countless others who were a part of caring for and welcoming Sophie and Dasah into the world, thank you for being a part of a beautiful story God was writing for our family. You have been like family to us!

Though so many were a part of making this book a reality, the story you have read could not have been lived or written without the support of the hundreds and thousands of people who have journeyed with us over the last six years. I must thank the army of men and women who have gathered around us to encourage, love, and support us in a season of deep loss. I have been able to mention many of your names, but there are still so many names I haven't and many names unknown to me. But know this—your prayers and your support have truly been multiplied in our lives, and my prayer is that it would continue to be multiplied as more people hear of what God has done in the pages of this book.

And finally, to you my readers, thank you for picking up this book, for sharing it with your friends, and for joining me in the journey of discovering who this God is who brings life out of death. He continues to meet me in the darkness, and I pray you will know Him as the same God who will meet you in your own season of darkness. It is a privilege to share with you my story and to perhaps in a small way be a part of yours.

# NOTES

## 1. The Death of Dreams

1. Hannah Hurnard, *Hinds' Feet on High Places* (Living Books, 1997), 66.

## 2. The Waiting Hope

1. James Strong, *Strong's Exhaustive Concordance* (Peabody, MA: Hendrickson, 2007).

2. Andrew Murray, *Waiting on God* (Conshohocken, PA: Infinity, 2015), 69.

## 3. The Darkness Begins

1. Lettie Cowman, *Streams in the Desert* (Grand Rapids, MI: Zondervan, 1965), 89.

2. "Facts about Anencephaly," Centers for Disease Control and Prevention, accessed June 20, 2018, www.cdc.gov/ncbddd/birthdefects/anencephaly.html.

3. "Pregnancy termination following prenatal diagnosis of anencephaly or spina bifida: a systematic review of the literature," National Center for Biotechnology Information, accessed June 20, 2018, www.ncbi.nlm.nih.gov/pmc/articles/PMC4589245/.

4. Elisabeth Elliot, *The Shaping of a Christian Family: How My Parents Nurtured My Faith* (Ada, MI: Revell, 2005), 178–79.

## 7. The Greatest Fairy Story

1. J. R. R. Tolkien, *The Letters of J. R. R. Tolkien* (Boston: Houghton Mifflin Harcourt, 1995), 100.

2. Verlyn Flieger and Douglas A. Anderson, eds., *Tolkien on Fairy-Stories* (Nashville: HarperCollins, 2014), 22.

## 9. The Coming Losses

1. Corrie ten Boom, et al., *The Hiding Place* (Peabody, MA: Hendrickson, 2015).

2. Bill Bright, *How You Can Walk in the Spirit* (Wayne, NJ: New Life, 1998).

3. James Strong, *Strong's Exhaustive Concordance* (Peabody, MA: Hendrickson, 2007).

4. Lettie Cowman, *Streams in the Desert* (Grand Rapids, MI: Zondervan, 1965).

## 11. The Explosion of Love

1. Now I Lay Me Down to Sleep is a nonprofit organization "providing the gift of remembrance photography for parents suffering the loss of a baby." You can find more information about them at www.nowilaymedowntosleep.org.

## 12. The Best Is Yet to Come

1. Nancy Tillman, *On the Night You Were Born* (Basingstoke, UK: Feiwel and Friends, 2017).

2. John Piper, "Ruth: The Best Is Yet to Come," Desiring God, July 22, 1984, www.desiringgod.org.

## 13. The Other Shoe Drops

1. David Guthrie, quoted in Randy Alcorn, *90 Days of God's Goodness: Daily Reflections That Shine Light on Personal Darkness* (New York: Multnomah, 2011), 213.

2. Hannah Hurnard, *Hinds' Feet on High Places* (Living Books, 1997), 173–74.

## 15. The Myrtle Tree

1. Verlyn Flieger and Douglas A. Anderson, eds., *Tolkien on Fairy-Stories* (Nashville: HarperCollins, 2014).

2. Amy Carmichael, *Gold by Moonlight* (Fort Washington, PA: CLC Publications, 1991), 74–75.

3. John Piper, "The Lost Need to See Your Joy," Desiring God, September 4, 2017, www.desiringgod.org.

## 16. The Lonely Places

1. Timothy S. Laniak, *While Shepherds Watch Their Flocks: Forty Daily Reflections on Biblical Leadership* (Charlotte, NC: ShepherdLeader, 2007), 172.

2. John Piper, "Sorrowful Yet Always Rejoicing," Desiring God, December 29, 2012, www.desiringgod.org.

## 19. The Lamenting Heart

1. C. S. Lewis, *The Complete C. S. Lewis Signature Classics* (San Francisco: HarperOne, 2007), 658.

2. C. H. Spurgeon, *The Treasury of David* (Peabody, MA: Hendrickson, 1988).

3. Dan Allender, "The Hidden Hope in Lament," *Mars Hill Review* 1 (1994): 25–38.

4. Elisabeth Elliot, *The Path of Loneliness: Finding Your Way Through the Wilderness to God* (Ada, MI: Revell, 2007), 32.

5. Edward Mote, "My Hope Is Built on Nothing Less," *The United Methodist Hymnal* (Nashville: The United Methodist Publishing House, 1989), 368.

## 20. The Unimaginable Hope

1. Quoted in Elisabeth Elliot, *The Path of Loneliness: Finding Your Way Through the Wilderness to God* (Ada, MI: Revell, 2007).

2. R. C. Sproul, *Be Still My Soul: Embracing God's Purpose and Provision in Suffering*, ed. Nancy Guthrie (Wheaton, IL: Crossway, 2010), 47.

3. Elisabeth Elliot, *Shadow of the Almighty: The Life & Testament of Jim Elliot* (New York: Harper & Row, 2011).

## Epilogue

1. David and Nancy Guthrie, *When Your Family's Lost a Loved One: Finding Hope Together* (Carol Stream, IL: Focus on the Family, 2008), 57–58.